LIFESKILLS™ HANDBOOKS

21st CENTURY

Everyday *Household Tasks*

Emily Hutchinson
and
Susan M. Freese

SADDLEBACK
EDUCATIONAL PUBLISHING

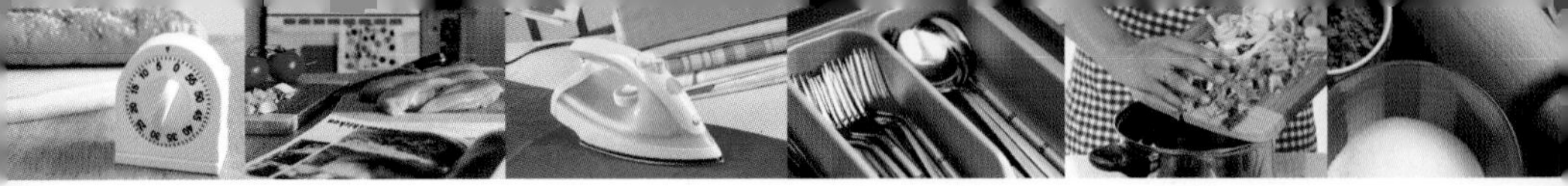

SADDLEBACK
EDUCATIONAL PUBLISHING
www.sdlback.com

ISBN-13: 978-1-61651-691-8
ISBN-10: 1-61651-691-7
eBook: 978-1-61247-343-7

Printed in Guangzhou, China
1111/CA21101811

16 15 14 13 12   1 2 3 4 5

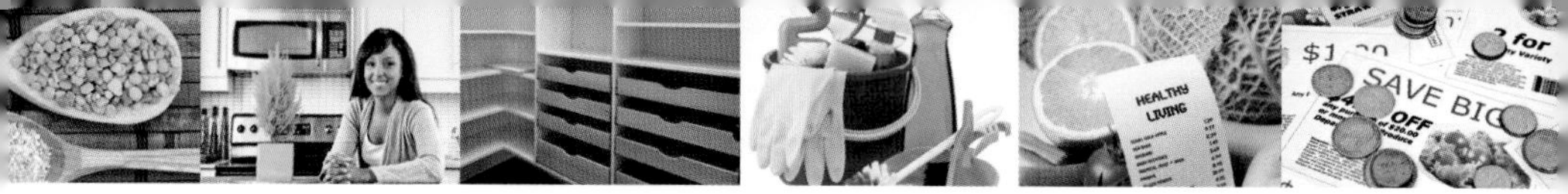

Contents

ATS

SECTION **1**

Grocery Shopping

Good grocery shoppers have a plan. They know exactly what they have at home, and they know exactly what they need from the store. They also know how to buy nutritious, high-quality food *and* save money. What do you need to learn to eat better and spend less on groceries?

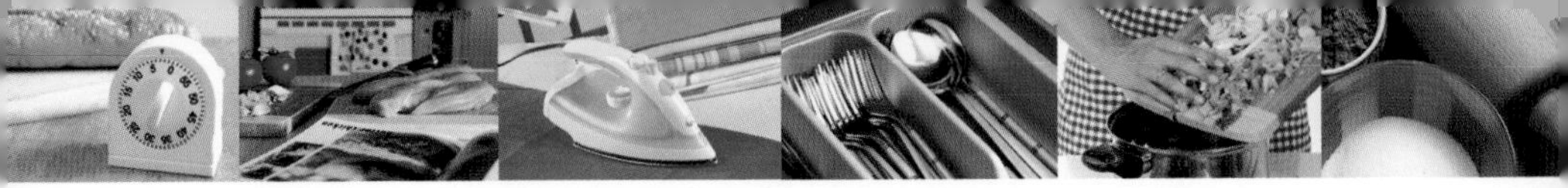

New Habits for a New Year

Most years, Kevin didn't think about making New Year's resolutions. But this year, he had a definite goal in mind: He wanted to get better at buying groceries.

Kevin's girlfriend thought he was being silly. "Who cares about buying groceries?" she asked. Kevin explained that he cared, for two reasons.

One reason was cost. Kevin knew he spent a lot of money at the grocery store. After all, he went there three or four times a week. He usually stopped on his way home from work. Yet it seemed he never had anything in the house to eat. He always had food, but none of it seemed to go together to make a meal.

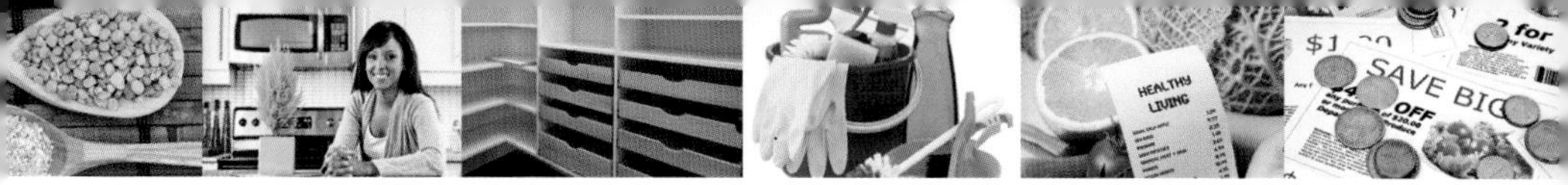

As a result, Kevin often ended up eating some of this and some of that. For instance, one night for dinner, he had a frozen burrito and a can of peaches. Other nights, he didn't bother trying to figure out what to eat. He just ordered a pizza instead!

Kevin's second concern was health. He knew he didn't have a healthy diet. He ate hardly any fresh fruits and vegetables. He didn't often buy them, because it took time to clean them and cook them. Plus, they spoiled if he didn't eat them right away.

Instead, Kevin ate a lot of ready-made foods, such as canned, boxed, and frozen products. He liked how fast and easy these foods were to prepare. Most of them, he just popped into the microwave. But he knew these foods weren't very good for him.

Kevin had developed some bad eating and shopping habits. He rarely thought about his meals in advance. And that meant he made a lot of trips to the grocery store. He needed a plan!

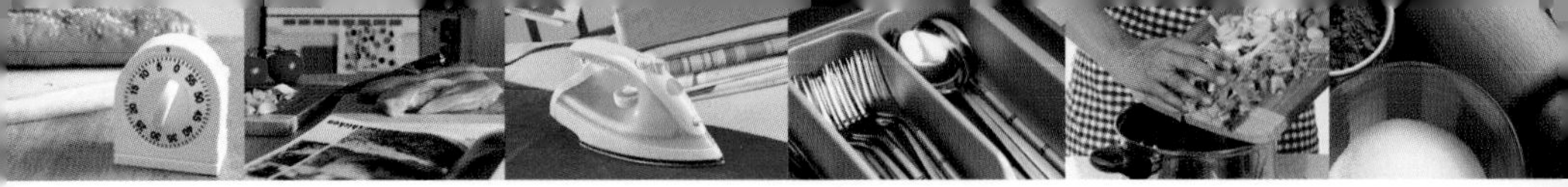

CHAPTER **1**

Buying Grocery Staples

Grocery staples are the basic food items you use again and again. They are the foods you need to have on hand to put together meals on a regular basis.

Guidelines for Good Eating

The US Department of Agriculture (USDA) has developed guidelines for a healthy diet. Look at the illustration on the next page, which is from the USDA's Web site: www.ChooseMyPlate.gov. This "plate" shows the

categories of foods you should eat every day and in what general amounts. Use this "plate" to help you decide what staples to keep in your kitchen.

Also visit the USDA's Web site for other helpful information on healthy eating. Learn what foods to limit in your diet. And get a personal food plan based on your age, gender, size, and activity level.

Categories
Types or groups.

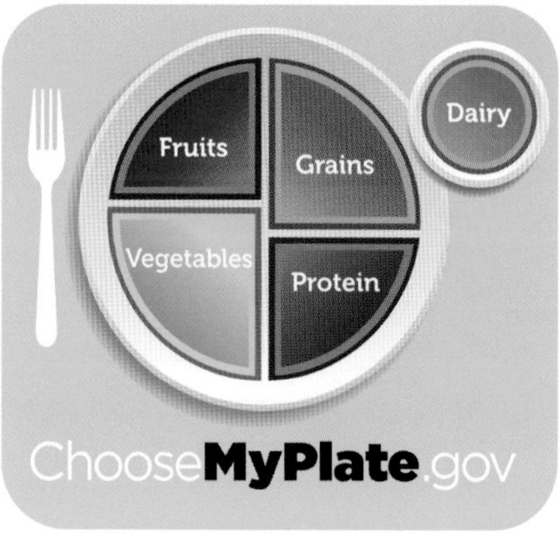

Storing Foods

As you might guess, some of the foods from the USDA "plate" should be stored in the refrigerator or freezer. Dairy products, such as milk and cheese, must be refrigerated.

Many canned and bottled foods must be refrigerated after they've been opened. Otherwise, they will spoil. Look for this requirement on the food's label.

Fresh fruits and vegetables can be stored in the refrigerator but don't have to be. So can grains, such as breads and muffins. These foods will generally last longer if kept cool.

Other foods should be stored in your pantry. A *pantry* is a cabinet, closet, or small room used for food storage. Foods stored in a pantry are often called *dry goods* and *canned goods*.

For all kinds of foods, pay attention to the ***expiration date***. Most food can still be eaten past this date, but it's quality and taste won't be as good.

Expiration date

The date after which something should no longer be used.

[FACT]

The Facts about Expiration Dates

Many people are surprised to learn that food isn't usually spoiled or harmful after its expiration date. It just won't taste as good, and the quality may not be as good.

Most people are also surprised to know that grocery stores don't have to remove foods from the shelves after their expiration dates. To avoid buying something old, you should check products' expiration dates while you shop. Look for these codes and know what they mean:

- **Sell by:** Don't buy a food after this date. This is the expiration date.
- **Best if used by:** The flavor or quality may be less after this date, but the food can still be eaten.
- **Use by:** This is the last day the food's manufacturer stands by its quality.

Other Staples to Have on Hand

Do you bake often? If so, staples for your kitchen should include baking supplies, such as flour, sugar, baking powder, baking soda, salt, and yeast.

Herbs and spices are also staples. Rosemary, oregano, thyme, cinnamon, and pepper all add flavor to food.

And what about ***condiments***? Products such as soy sauce, ketchup, mustard, mayonnaise, and barbecue sauce are staples, too.

Shopping for Staples

When you shop, always be aware of how long a product will stay fresh. Fresh fruits and vegetables can't be stored for very long. But canned and frozen fruits and vegetables can be stored for quite some time.

You can buy enough canned and frozen foods to fill up your pantry and your freezer. But you should buy only as much fresh food as you can eat in a few days.

Condiments

Sauces and other toppings that add flavor to food. Condiments are generally put on the table and used by individuals to flavor their own food.

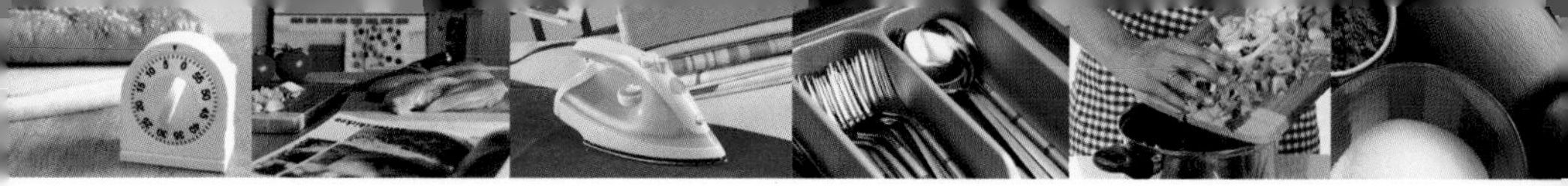

Setting Up Your Pantry

The goods in your pantry should be organized in a logical way. That will make it a lot easier to find things.

For example, it's a good idea to keep pasta and pasta sauces next to each other. You might also group things such as cereals, baking ingredients, and related canned goods. Figure out your own plan, and then follow it!

[FACT]

New USDA Food Guidelines

For many years, the USDA has provided Americans with guidelines for healthy eating. In 2010, the model for those guidelines changed from a "pyramid" to a "plate." Although the basic food groups stayed the same, the suggested amounts changed.

What was the main reason for the change? Too many Americans are overweight.

To control your weight, follow two simple guidelines:

1. Eat less.
2. Move more.

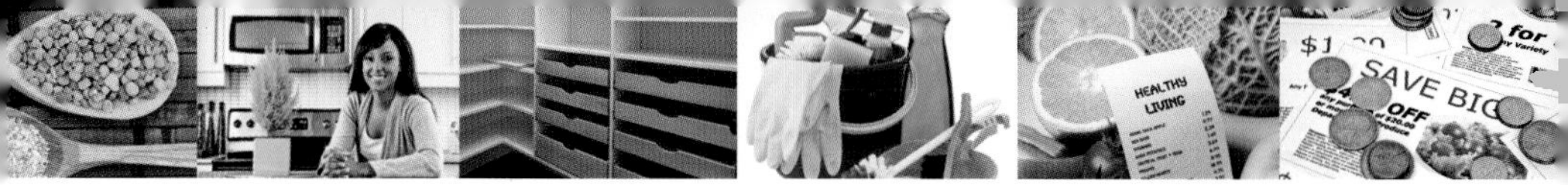

[FACT]

What Is the USDA?

The US Department of Agriculture (USDA) is one of 15 government departments that advise the US president. The USDA provides advice on food, agriculture, natural resources, and related topics. It has a wide range of responsibilities:

- Giving financial help to farmers
- Making plans and policies for agriculture
- Funding agricultural research
- Overseeing international trade of crops
- Providing food safety
- Educating Americans about food and nutrition
- Protecting the national forests
- Managing natural resources

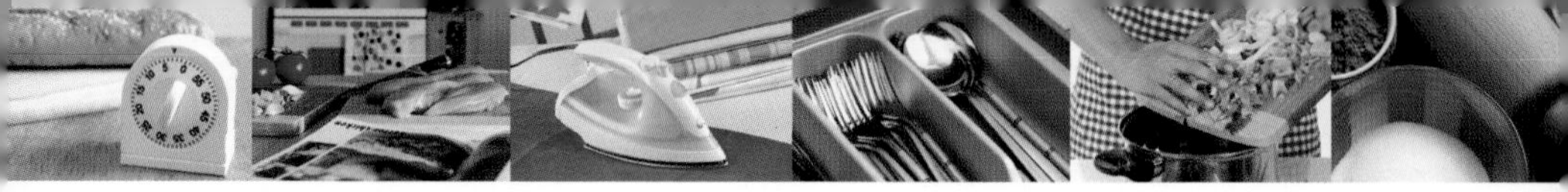

CHAPTER **2**

Reading Grocery Ads

Lissa has been looking at grocery store advertisements, or ads. She knows that ***comparison shopping*** will help her get the best bargains she can.

Here are two different ads she saw in the local newspaper this morning:

[FACT]

Stores That Sell Groceries

- **Markets** are small stores that are often one-of-a-kind. Some sell certain kinds of foods, such as ethnic foods. Prices at markets may be higher than elsewhere, but the quality and selection are usually excellent.
- **Convenience stores** sell grocery staples, snack foods, and a variety of other items. However, the selection will be limited, and the prices will be higher.
- **Grocery stores** are often found in small communities and locally owned. They offer a full selection of foods plus some household items. Prices are usually higher than at larger stores. But coupons are often offered in the local newspaper.
- **Supermarkets** are chains of big grocery stores that operate throughout a region. Because of their large size, supermarkets tend to have lower prices than other stores. They also tend to advertise a lot and provide coupons.
- **Discount stores and warehouse stores** sell many things in addition to groceries. But all of their products tend to be sold at lower prices than found elsewhere. Warehouse stores usually require buying in large quantities.

Comparison shop

To check the price of the same product at several different stores. The goal is to find the best price before making a purchase.

Lissa also looks through the newspaper for ***coupons***. She uses them to help her save money on certain products.

Coupon

A kind of ticket that allows buying an item at a lower price.

[FACT]

Where to Find Grocery Store Coupons

- **Sunday newspaper:** Cut out coupons from the inserts that contain grocery store ads.
- **Internet:** Print out coupons from Web sites such as Coupons.com, Redplum .com, and SmartSource .com.
- **Manufacturers' Web sites:** If you have favorite products, check the manufacturers' Web sites for coupons.
- **Grocery store aisles:** Look for small machines that print out coupons. Also look for tear-off pads of coupons.
- **Women's magazines:** Every issue of the magazine *All You* contains coupons that provide large savings.
- **Food packages:** Look on the backs and insides of packages, where coupons are sometimes printed.
- **Customer service desk:** Ask for coupon books and store coupons. Some also may be found at the store's Web site.

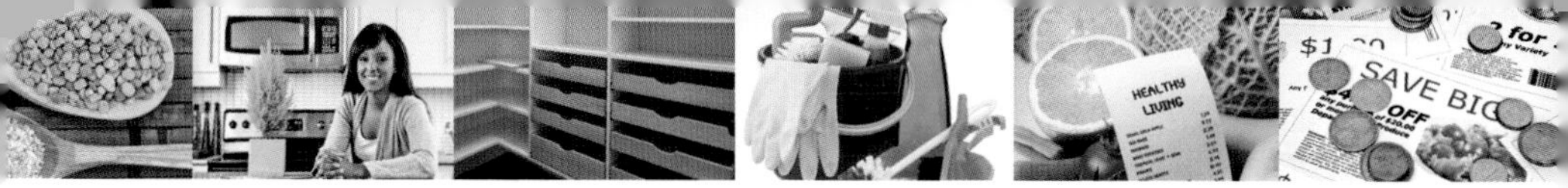

How Do Coupons Work?

Coupons are like money. You give them to the cashier when you check out and pay for your groceries. The value of each coupon is subtracted from what you owe.

But in most cases, coupons can be used only to buy specific things. For instance, a coupon for laundry detergent will be good only for a particular kind of laundry detergent. And in many cases, the coupon also requires buying a particular size or number of items.

Coupons also have expiration dates. Most stores won't take coupons past these dates.

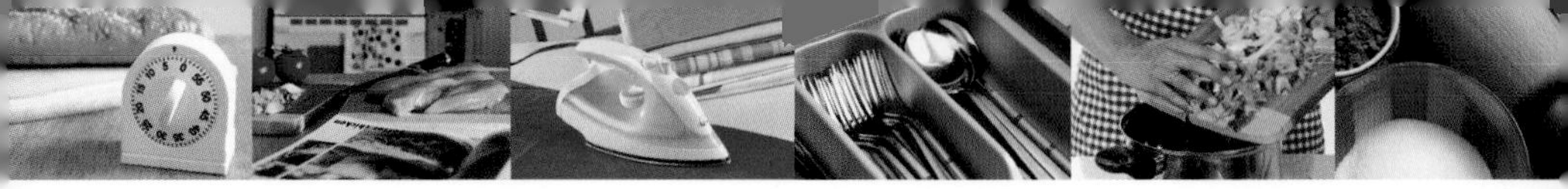

Learn What Experienced Shoppers Know

Lissa decided to go to Smart Mart to do her grocery shopping. She liked the price on the blue cheese salad dressing. She'd never seen it so low! Her mother called this kind of low-priced item a "loss leader." The store sold the product at a loss just to get customers to come in.

When Lissa arrived at the store, she saw a sign posted on a display just inside the door. The sign was for a display of canned tuna. The sign was handmade, so the sale seemed to have occurred suddenly.

Lissa hadn't seen this special in the morning newspaper ad. She figured the store must have gotten a good buy on the tuna. And it wanted to pass on the savings to its customers. This seemed like another good buy! Lissa put six cans into her cart.

But in the aisle where tuna was regularly sold, Lissa noticed that Brand Y tuna was selling for 89¢. She compared the two brands of tuna, side by side. Both were chunk light tuna and packed in water. And both cans were the same weight. Lissa put six cans of Brand Y tuna into her cart. She put the Brand X tuna back where she found it.

Lissa remembered something else her mother had told her. A "special" may or may not be a good deal. A sign that says the price is 99¢ "today only" suggests the price will be *higher* tomorrow. But the

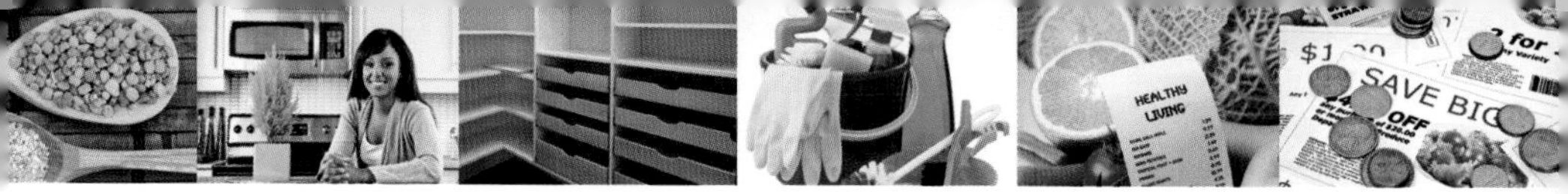

price might be *lower* tomorrow! Careful shoppers always compare prices, no matter what a sign says.

When Lissa got to the yogurt display, she put five containers in her cart. She knew that just because the sign says "10 for $5," you don't have to buy 10. The items are 50¢ each, no matter how many you buy. Of course, the store wants you to buy a lot—but you don't have to.

Lissa remembered she had a coupon for another brand of yogurt, but she decided not to use it. It required buying 10 containers, which was more than she wanted.

Tips for Shopping with Coupons

- Collect coupons only for items you normally buy.
- Don't use coupons to buy name-brand items that cost more than store-brand items.
- Find out if your store has certain days when it doubles the value of coupons.
- Don't use coupons that require you to buy more of something than you'll use.
- Organize coupons by category in an envelope or file.
- Once a month, go through your collection of coupons and throw out the ones that have expired.
- Have the coupons you plan to use ready before you get to the checkout to pay for your groceries.
- Make sure the cashier rings up coupon items correctly.

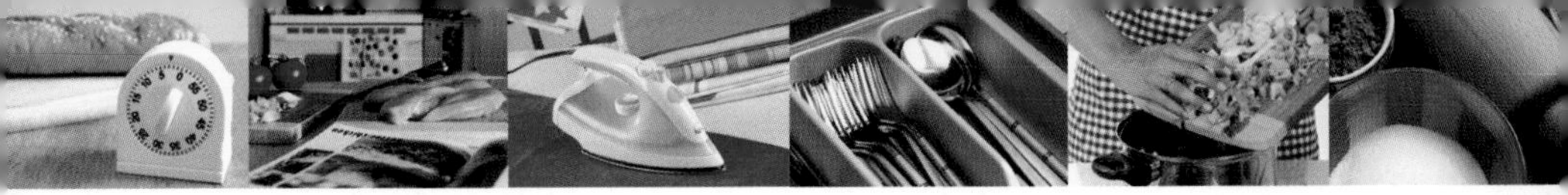

CHAPTER 3

Planning Meals

Do you plan meals for your whole household, you and someone else, or just for yourself? In any case, you need to think about two topics to plan wisely: ***nutrition*** and ***variety***.

Nutrition

The act or process of getting the foods needed for health and growth.

Variety

Difference or choice.

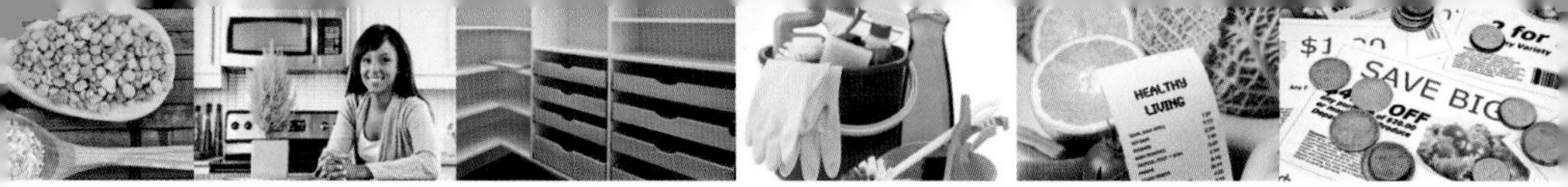

Nutrition

Remember the USDA's "plate" diagram in Chapter 1? It contains five categories of foods. For those categories, the USDA provides these easy-to-remember tips:

1. **Grains: "Make at least half your grains whole."**
   Whole grains include oats, brown rice, bulgur, barley, and rye. White breads, rices, and flours have fewer health benefits.
2. **Vegetables: "Vary your veggies."**
   Choose a mix of colors of vegetables: green, red, orange, and yellow. Different-colored vegetables have different health benefits.

3. **Fruits: "Focus on fruits."**
   Eat fresh fruit as much as possible, rather than canned or frozen. And drink 100% fruit juice, not sugar-flavored fruit drinks.

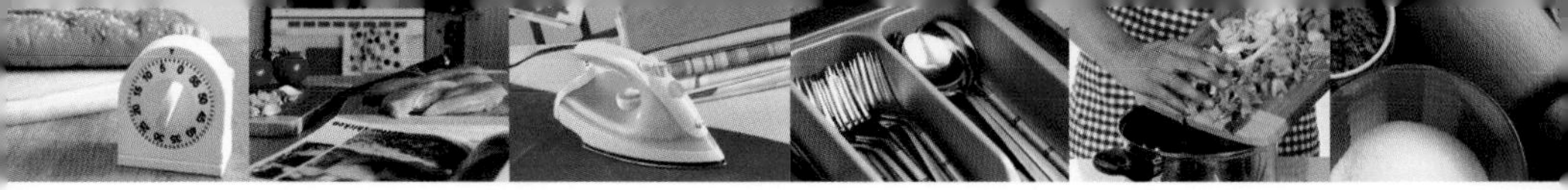

4. **Dairy: “Get your calcium-rich foods.”**

   Calcium is important for building strong bones. Switch to fat-free or low-fat dairy products.

5. **Protein: “Go lean with protein.”**

   Meat is a good source of protein. But look for lean, low-fat cuts of meat. Beans and nuts are also good sources of protein.

   The USDA also ***recommends*** eating more and less of certain foods:

Eat More of These Foods

- Fruits and vegetables
- Whole-grain breads and other grains
- Fat-free or low-fat milk
- Water

Recommend

To suggest or propose.

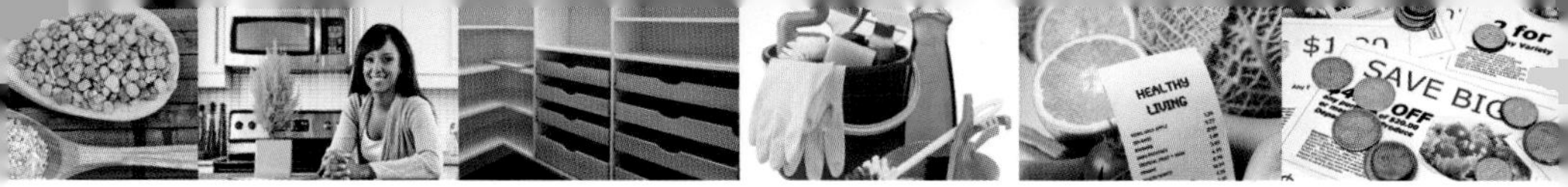

Eat Less of These Foods

- Canned, boxed, and frozen foods
- Sugary drinks, such as soda and fruit-based beverages

[FACT]

Reading Nutrition Labels

Packaged foods have nutrition labels. Learn to read them to determine three things:

1. **What's the serving size?** Check out how much is considered one serving—for example, ¼ cup. The other information on the label is based on that serving size.
2. **What's in it?** Check out what's good for you: vitamins, calcium, and fiber. Also check out what's bad for you: saturated (solid) fat and sodium (salt).
3. **Is it right for you?** Judge if the food is a good choice for you. If it's not particularly healthy but you'd like to have it, then take a smaller serving.

Nutrition Facts

Serving Size 1/4 Cup (30g)
Servings Per Container About 38

Amount Per Serving	
Calories 200	Calories from Fat 150
	% Daily Value*
Total Fat 17g	**26**%
Saturated Fat 2.5g	**13**%
Trans Fat 0g	
Cholesterol 0mg	**0**%
Sodium 120mg	**5**%
Total Carbohydrate 7g	**2**%
Dietary Fiber 2g	**8**%
Sugars 1g	
Protein 5g	
Vitamin A 0% •	Vitamin C 0%
Calcium 4% •	Iron 8%

*Percent Daily Values are based on a 2,000 calorie diet

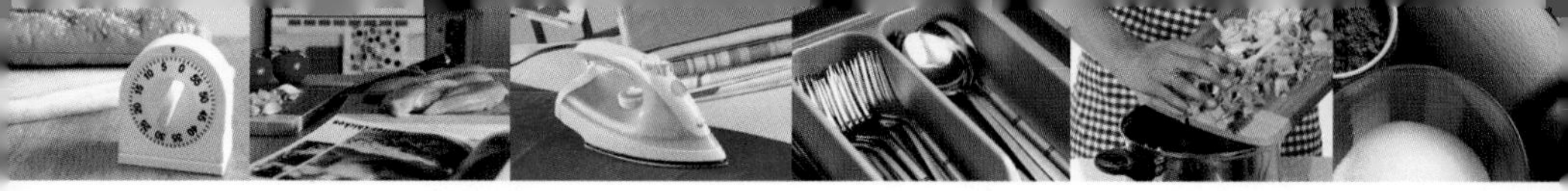

[FACT]

Ingredients Label

Packaged foods also have ingredients labels. The ingredients are listed in order from largest to smallest amount or quantity. Again, learn to read these labels and determine what they mean:

- **Whole grains:** Products with terms like *whole grain* and *multi-grain* in their names may be advertising falsely. To find out, see whether a whole grain (not just wheat or flour) comes first in the list of ingredients.
- **Sugars:** Avoid products with added sugars, especially sucrose and corn syrup.
- **Sodium (salt):** A small quantity can still be a lot. Look for a very low percentage. Also look for products said to be "low sodium."
- **Good fats:** Most oils are good for you. (*Oils* are fats that are liquid at room temperature.) Oils come from vegetables, seeds, and nuts.
- **Bad fats:** Solid fats, which come from animal foods, are usually bad for you. (They include butter, cream, lard, and fat from meat.) Other bad fats are found in stick margarine and a few oils (coconut, palm, and palm kernel).

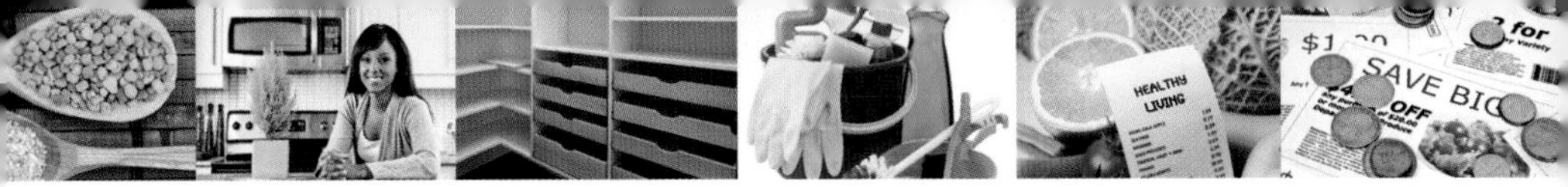

Variety

It's no fun to eat the same thing every day. We all like a little variety in our meals. Smart meal planners try to think of different kinds of foods that meet the USDA recommendations.

Visit the USDA's Web site for suggestions on meal planning, including menu ideas (www.ChooseMyPlate.gov). Also learn about planning meals for children, vegetarians, and others with special diets.

If you can, plan a week's worth of meals in advance. And shop for groceries using a list. Your list should include all the items you'll need to make the meals you've planned for the week.

As you make your grocery list, check what you already have in the refrigerator, freezer, and pantry. Add to the list any items you don't have.

Rules to Eat By

Remember these two general meal-planning recommendations from the USDA:

1. Enjoy your food, but eat less.
2. Avoid oversized portions.
   Also remember the words of Michael Pollan from his book *In Defense of Food*:
   "Eat food. Not too much. Mostly plants."

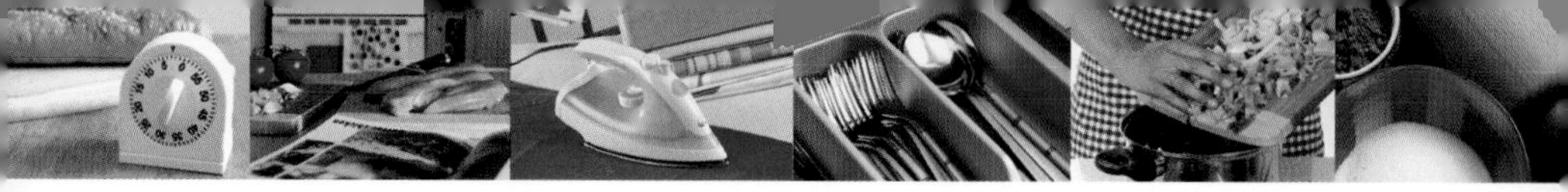

CHAPTER **4**

Getting the Best Value

Most people don't like to waste things, especially money. But being ***thrifty*** doesn't come naturally to everyone.

You can learn how to be a thrifty grocery shopper. For instance, wise shoppers know what to buy at different kinds of stores: discount stores and warehouse clubs, supermarkets, and markets.

Thrifty
Careful and smart with money.

How to Get the Most for Your Money

Follow these tips to get the best value for your money:

1. **Make a grocery list.** Begin writing down the ingredients you need to make specific recipes. But when you shop, be willing to consider other possibilities. For example, if fish is on your list, don't insist on halibut if you see some nice cod on sale. Also try to buy ***sustainable*** fish. In addition, keep variety in mind. If you've written down "salad stuff," don't always get the same things. When you can, buy locally grown ***produce***.

Sustainable

Produced or operated without harming the environment.

Produce

Products from farms and gardens. Generally, the word *produce* is used to mean fresh fruits and vegetables.

[FACT]

Fresh Produce All Year

If you live in an area that has cold winters, you can't buy locally grown produce throughout the year. But thanks to refrigerated shipping, you can buy your favorite fruits and vegetables even in winter. This produce comes from countries near Earth's equator, which are always warm. It also comes from places far south of the equator. The seasons there are opposite the seasons in North America.

Most year-round produce comes from Mexico and countries in Central and South America. For example, tomatoes, eggplant, bell peppers, squash, and cucumbers are shipped from Mexico. And grapes, avocadoes, berries, peaches, plums, and nectarines are shipped from Chile.

2. **Don't shop when you're hungry.** When you're hungry, you're much more likely to buy food items you don't need. And you're more likely to buy ready-made foods, which aren't usually the best value.

3. **Use coupons.** But when you shop, bring only the coupons you know you're going to need. Don't buy things you don't need just to save a few cents.

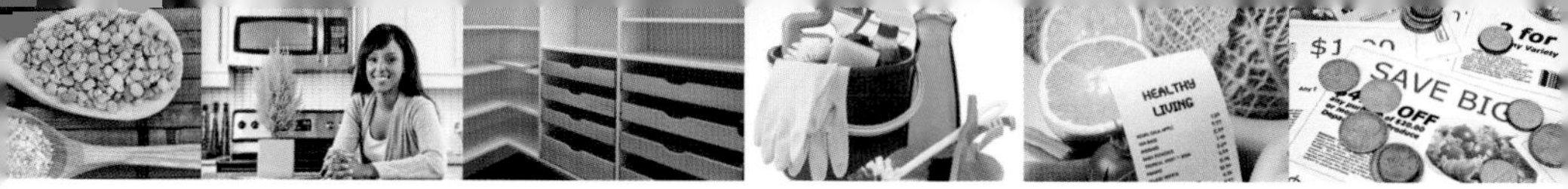

4. **Don't go up and down every aisle.** In most supermarkets, the fresh foods are placed around the edges of the store—on the sides and in the back. The middle aisles are lined with ready-made foods, chips, sodas, ice cream, and nonfood items.

5. **Look at the top and bottom shelves.** If you must shop in the middle aisles, look at the top and bottom shelves there. That's where you'll usually find the best bargains. Why? The average supermarket shopper is a woman about 5' 4" tall. The most expensive products are displayed at her eye level—on the middle shelves.

6. **Read and compare labels.** Study the list of ingredients to see what you're getting for your money. Don't be fooled by fancy product names and package designs.

7. **Don't be a slave to name-brand products.** There's a reason the name brands cost more than the store brands. That reason is advertising! It costs a lot of money to advertise products on TV. Store-brand products are usually of equal quality but cost much less.

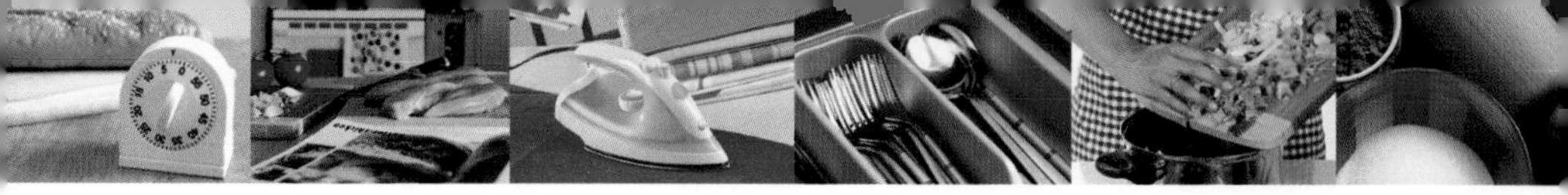

8. **Shop for seasonal foods.** If you buy produce that's out of season where you live, it will be more expensive. That's because it had to be shipped from a distance. You can also grow some ***seasonal*** fruits, vegetables, and herbs inexpensively in your own garden or in pots on your porch.

9. **Use unit pricing.** Unit pricing lets you compare the costs of different products in equal amounts. For example, suppose you see two bottles of juice. One is $3.49, and the other is $2.69. Don't assume that the lower-priced bottle is the best buy. It might contain half the amount of juice as the other bottle. To get the best value, figure out the cost per unit, such as per ounce or per quart. Sometimes, the unit price is provided with the product information on the edge of the shelf at the store. If not, figure out the unit price for yourself.

Seasonal
Available only at a certain time of year.

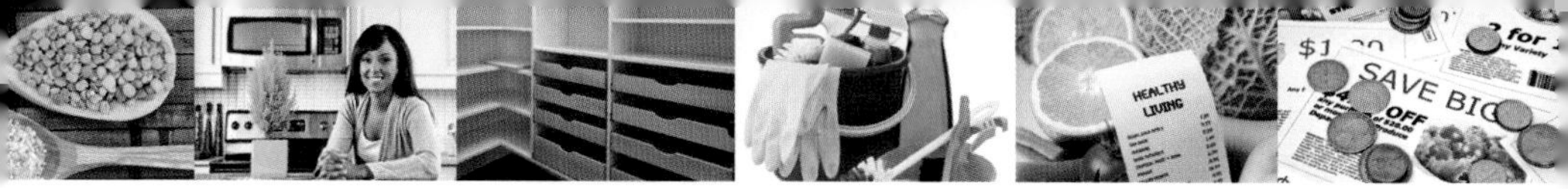

[FACT]

When's the Best Time to Buy Produce?

	Vegetables	Fruits
Spring	artichokes asparagus avocadoes baby lettuces carrots new potatoes peas (snow, garden, sugar snap) radishes scallions spinach	apricots cherries rhubarb strawberries
Summer	beets bell peppers broccoli corn cucumbers eggplant green beans summer squash tomatoes	blackberries blueberries nectarines peaches plums raspberries watermelons
Fall	broccoli brussels sprouts butternut squash cauliflower leeks mushrooms potatoes sweet potatoes	apples figs grapes pears pomegranates
Winter	acorn squash cabbage collard greens fennel kale parsnips radicchio swiss chard turnips	grapefruit lemons oranges tangerines

SECTION **2**

Cooking

Television cooking shows make being in the kitchen look glamorous. But in real life, cooking involves fixing several meals a day—every day. To do that, you need to set up your kitchen with the right tools and equipment. You also need to know how to use a cookbook and follow a recipe. Having these basic supplies and skills will help you be a good cook and enjoy your time in the kitchen.

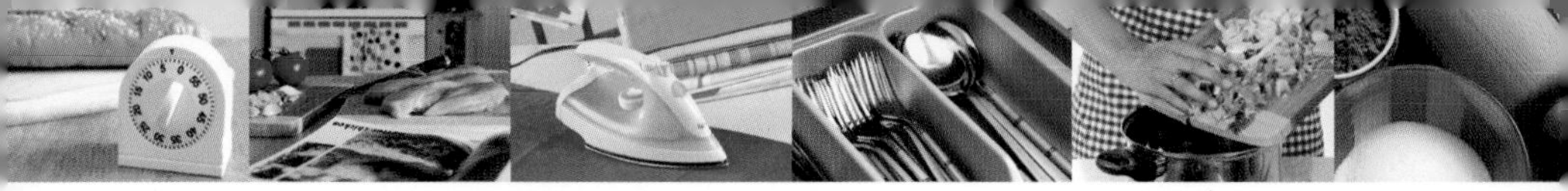

The Newest Cook in the Family

Maria had grown up around cooks and cooking. Everyone in her family liked to cook—men and women. And because of that, the family always had fantastic get-togethers. Maria looked forward to someday having those get-togethers at her house.

In fact, it wouldn't be long before Maria would have her first apartment. She'd be done with nursing school next year. After that, she planned on getting a job in the city and moving there.

Until then, Maria would stay living at home with her family. She liked helping her parents fix dinner, and they appreciated having her help. They were both busy with their jobs and their younger children's school

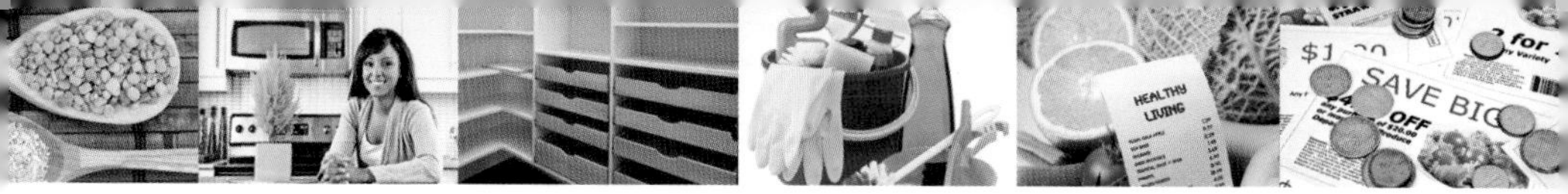

and sports activities. Plus, Maria knew they sometimes got tired of having to put a meal on the table.

Maria's grandmother had given her a cookbook for her birthday. The two of them had made several of the recipes in it. Working with her grandmother, Maria had learned a lot about using a cookbook and following a recipe. Her grandmother had also given her a lot of good tips from her years of experience in the kitchen.

Maria had even started to collect some of the tools and equipment she'd need for her own kitchen. Her parents had given her their old pots and pans after they bought new ones. And Maria had bought some mixing bowls and bakeware at a neighborhood garage sale.

Maria knew it would take a while to get all of the supplies and equipment she needed. But that was OK. In the meantime, she was enjoying her role as the newest cook in the family.

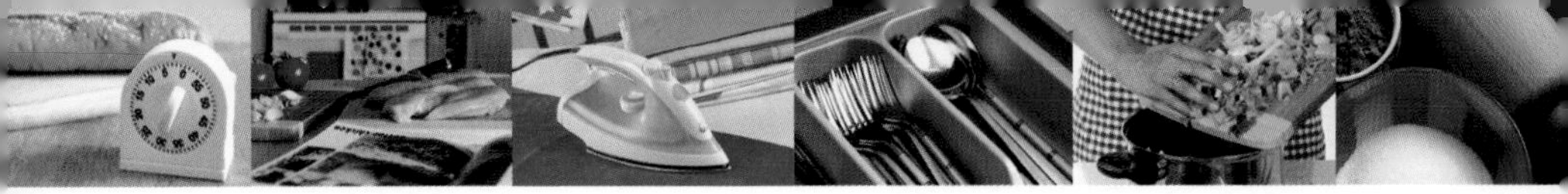

CHAPTER **1**

Setting Up a Kitchen

You're not ready to cook if you don't have the right tools. A well-equipped kitchen has a basic set of ***utensils***, pots and pans, bakeware, storage products, and ***gadgets***.

Utensils

Tools.

Gadgets

Clever or useful devices.

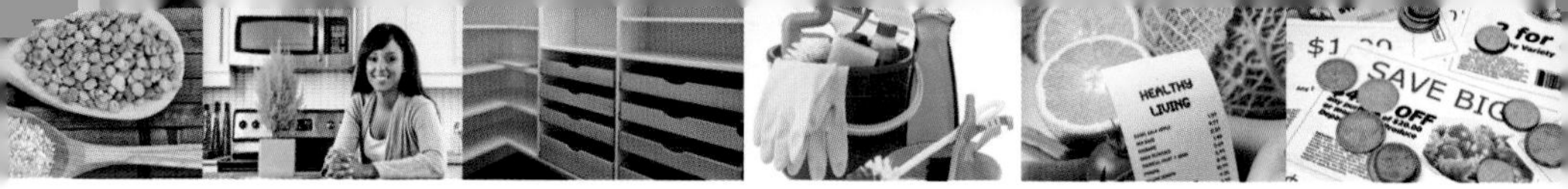

Utensils

- Mixing bowls of different sizes
- Dry measuring cups
- Clear-glass liquid measuring cup
- Measuring spoons
- Wooden spoons
- Rubber spatulas
- Flexible metal spatulas
- Variety of knives
- Sharpening steel for knives
- Vegetable peeler
- Long-handled fork
- Long-handled spoon
- Ladle
- Slotted spoon
- Tongs
- Kitchen scissors
- Pizza cutter
- Bottle opener
- Can opener
- Grater and/or shredder
- Small and large strainers
- Colander
- Kitchen timer
- Cutting board (plastic)
- Rolling pin
- Meat thermometer
- Oven thermometer
- Wire cooling rack
- Vegetable steamer

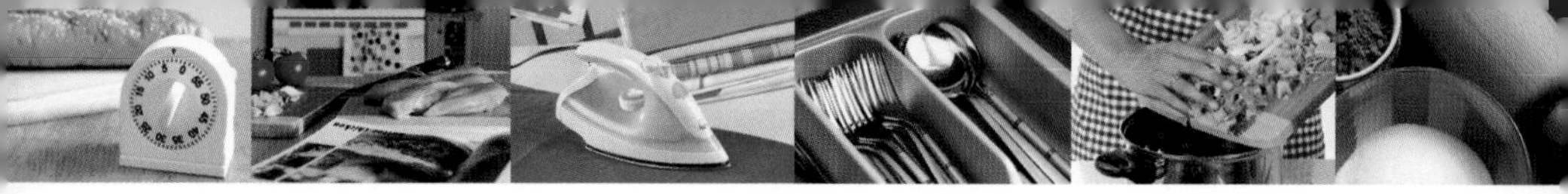

Cleaning Utensils: Wood versus Plastic

Many kitchen utensils are made of wood or plastic. Knowing the differences in how to clean them will make your utensils last longer.

Wood Utensils

- Wash utensils in the sink with warm, soapy water. Then rinse and dry with a clean towel.
- Don't soak utensils in water or put them in the dishwasher. Doing so will make the wood warp or crack.
- To protect against cracking, wipe utensils with a food-grade mineral oil.
- Store utensils in a dry, clean location.

Plastic Utensils

- Wash utensils by hand or in the dishwasher.
- If utensils need soaking to get them clean, put them in warm, soapy water.
- If needed, scrub utensils with a nylon scrubbing pad. Don't use a metal pad, which will scratch the utensils.
- To remove white spots (calcium deposits), wipe utensils with vinegar. Then rinse and dry. Don't clean utensils with ammonia or bleach.
- Store utensils in a dry, clean location.

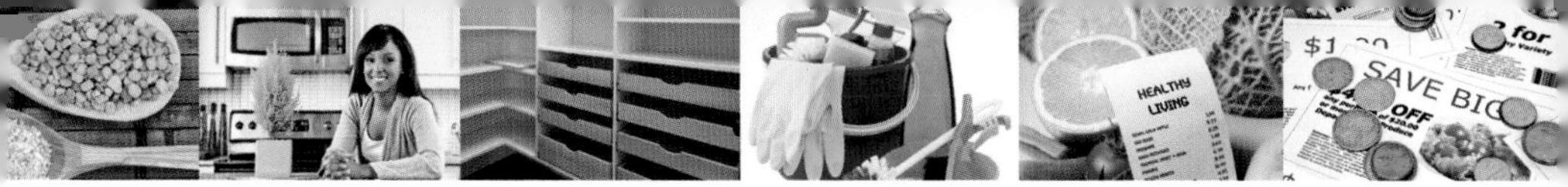

Buy a Basic Set of Knives

- **Chef's knife:** A chef's knife is long and wide. It's used for cutting, chopping, and slicing. Choose a knife with an 8- or 10-inch blade. Also look for a knife with a stainless steel blade. Keep the knife sharp by using a sharpening steel.
- **Utility knife:** A utility knife has a thin blade about 6 inches long. It has a wide range of uses in and out of the kitchen.
- **Paring knife:** A paring knife is similar to a chef's knife but smaller. The blade is usually 3 or 4 inches long. A paring knife is used for peeling and making other small cuts.
- **Serrated knife:** A serrated knife has small grooves in the blade and often a jagged edge. These features allow it to slice easily through bread and other soft foods without tearing them. Choose a serrated knife with a blade 6 to 8 inches long.

Pots and Pans

- 1-, 2-, and 3-quart covered saucepans
- 12- or 16-quart covered stock pot
- 4- or 6-quart covered Dutch oven
- 6- or 8-inch skillet
- 10-inch skillet
- 12-inch skillet
- Wok
- Roasting pan with rack
- Pizza pan
- Teakettle

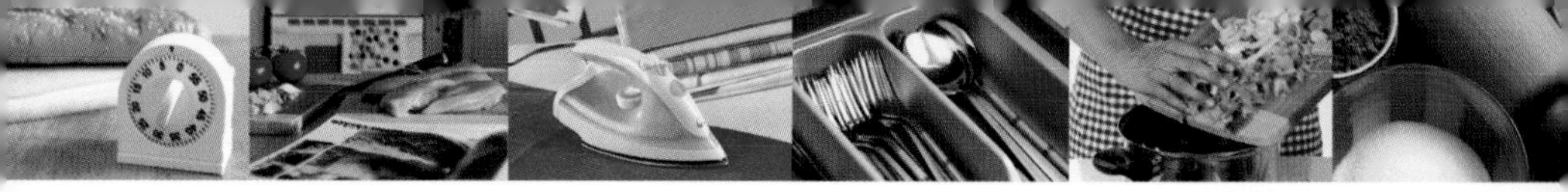

Choosing a Stove: Gas or Electric?

Experienced cooks usually have strong opinions about what type of stove they like. Here are some of their reasons for preferring gas or electric:

Gas

- A gas stove provides even heat. Also, the amount of heat can be changed immediately by turning the flame up or down.
- A gas stove heats quickly, so it saves energy.
- Gas is less expensive than electricity, so gas stoves are less expensive to operate.
- Unlike an electric stove, a gas stove can be used in a power failure.

Electric

- An electric stove is less expensive to purchase than a gas stove.
- Electric stoves are easy to clean.
- Electric stoves are safer than gas stoves in terms of fire hazards.
- No special set-up is required to operate an electric stove.

Bakeware

- → Cookie sheets
- → Custard cups or ramekins
- → Muffin tins
- → Pie plates
- → Loaf pans
- → Baking dishes
- → Cake pans

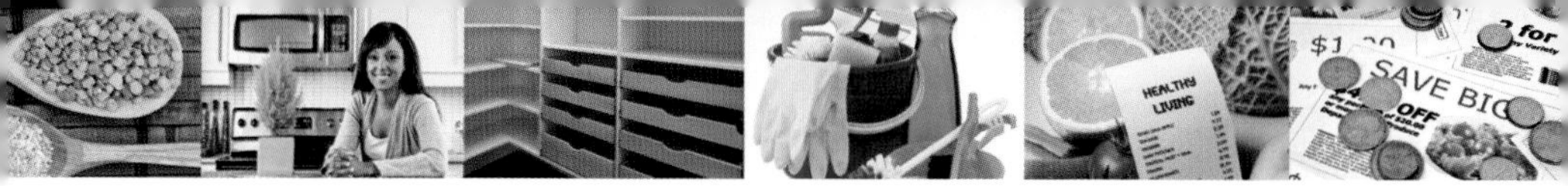

Food Storage Products

- Containers/Canisters
- Foil
- Clear plastic wrap
- Waxed paper
- Parchment paper
- Plastic bags (large and small)
- Juice pitcher

Useful Gadgets

- Blender
- Food processor
- Coffee maker
- Juicer
- Rice cooker
- Toaster
- Bread-making machine

Getting What You Need

You don't have to buy all these items at once. Start with the items that are most necessary for you. Go back through the lists, and think about how you'd use each item.

You also don't have to buy all these items brand new. You can find many of them at garage sales and estate sales or at second-hand stores. You will pay a ***fraction*** of the cost of buying them new.

There are a few other items that might not be on the list above. Special things you'll need to cook or bake your favorite dishes with. One of the most important items you'll definitely need is a set of potholders!

Fraction

A small amount or part of something.

CHAPTER **2**

Using a Cookbook

A good cookbook contains much more than recipes! It also contains a lot of useful information about meal planning, nutrition, and cooking ***techniques***.

Technique

A method or system for doing something.

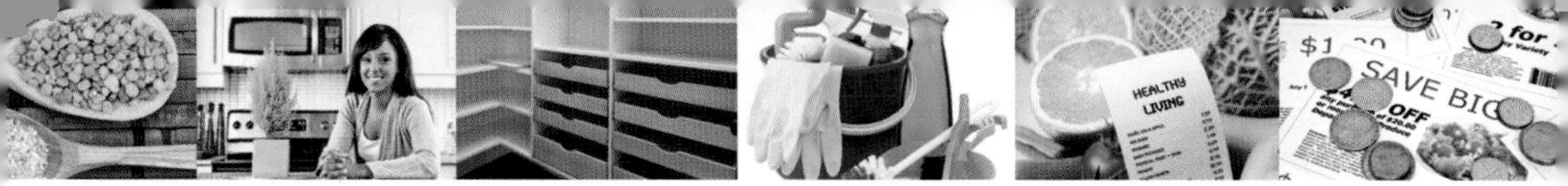

Cookbooks for Beginners

Cooking on your own for the first time can be challenging! Having a good cookbook will help get you through even the toughest of times.

These cookbooks include just about anything you'll need to know:

- ***Good Housekeeping***: This cookbook includes beginning information on topics such as how to read a recipe.
- ***Betty Crocker***: This cookbook comes in a three-ring binder, which allows easy access to recipes and other information.
- ***Pillsbury Complete Cookbook***: This cookbook also comes in a three-ring binder. And it contains many award-winning Pillsbury Bake-Off contest recipes.
- ***The All-New Ultimate Southern Living Cookbook***: This book includes many recipes and ideas for entertaining. It also includes a lot of photographs.

How a Cookbook Is Organized

To find that helpful information, you need to know how a cookbook is organized.

Like other books, most cookbooks are divided into chapters. In a cookbook, most of the chapters are about different types of foods. And some chapters may be about different types of meals, such as breakfast or a barbecue.

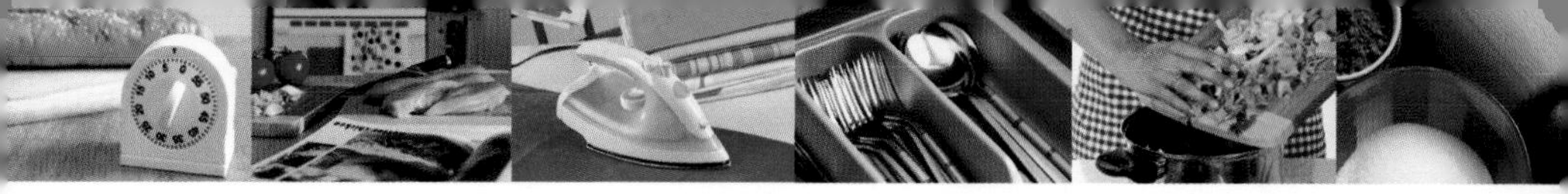

Other chapters may be about special topics. For instance, many cookbooks have chapters on nutrition and low fat cooking and eating.

Finally, cookbooks usually have information that will be helpful while you're cooking. This information is often provided at the end of the book. For example, many cookbooks have charts of equal measurements and ingredient replacements or substitutions.

[FACT]

Common Measurement Conversions

Do you know how many ounces are in a cup? Or how many cups are in a quart? To make sure you use the right amounts, look in your cookbook for a chart like this:

This Amount	Equals This . . .	. . . and This
1 teaspoon	1/6 fluid ounce	1/3 tablespoon
1 tablespoon	1/2 fluid ounce	3 teaspoons
1/8 cup	1 fluid ounce	2 tablespoons
1/4 cup	2 fluid ounces	4 tablespoons
1/3 cup	2 2/3 fluid ounces	1/4 cup + 4 teaspoons
1/2 cup	4 fluid ounces	8 tablespoons
1 cup	8 fluid ounces	1/2 pint
1 pint	16 fluid ounces	2 cups
1 quart	32 fluid ounces	2 pints
1 liter	34 fluid ounces	1 quart + 1/4 cup
1 gallon	128 fluid ounces	4 quarts

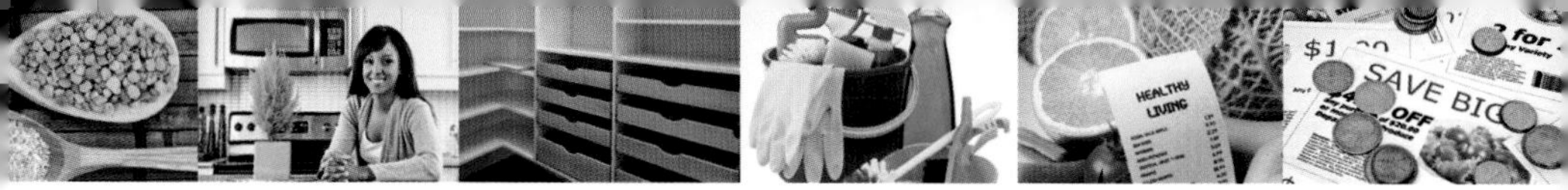

Many cookbooks have glossaries, too, which list and define cooking terms and techniques. And many cookbooks have indexes, which list types of foods and even names of specific recipes.

Review the Table of Contents

You can get a good ***overview*** of a cookbook by looking at its table of contents. Here's a sample table of contents:

> **Overview**
> An outline or summary.

Table of Contents

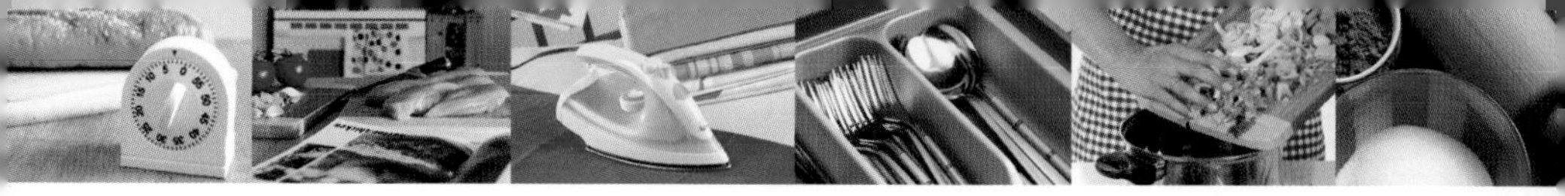

Go to Your Cookbook for Answers

Use your cookbook to find answers to questions about many things related to cooking and food.

Online Tools

Another useful source of information about cooking is the Internet. Web sites are available about everything from online cooking classes to special kitchen equipment.

One of the most useful online tools helps you find and organize recipes. Many Web sites offer lists of recipes. You can search them by the name of the recipe or the main ingredients it contains. At many sites, you can also select from a list of recipes and save your favorites. And when you find something you want to make, you can print out the recipe or save it on your computer.

Suppose you want to find out how caffeine affects the body. In the sample cookbook, you might find that information in Chapter 14, Nutrition Facts, on page 207. Maybe you want to find out how much fat is in one-half cup of Monterey jack cheese. You could turn to Chapter 15, Common Foods Analyzed, on page 215.

"Celebrity Chefs"

The Food Network is a television channel with programs about food and cooking. And the stars of these programs have come to be known as "celebrity chefs." Popular chefs include Wolfgang Puck, Paula Deen, and Emeril Lagasse. They appear on TV every day and have developed loyal audiences of viewers. In addition to TV shows, many of these chefs have their own cookbooks, magazines, cookware, and restaurants.

Suppose a recipe calls for *blanching*, and you're not sure what that term means. You could probably find out by looking it up in the Glossary of Cooking Techniques and Terms, which begins on page 225.

Or maybe you'd like to some new ideas for ways to cook potatoes. You could find recipes and their page numbers by looking up *Potatoes* in the index.

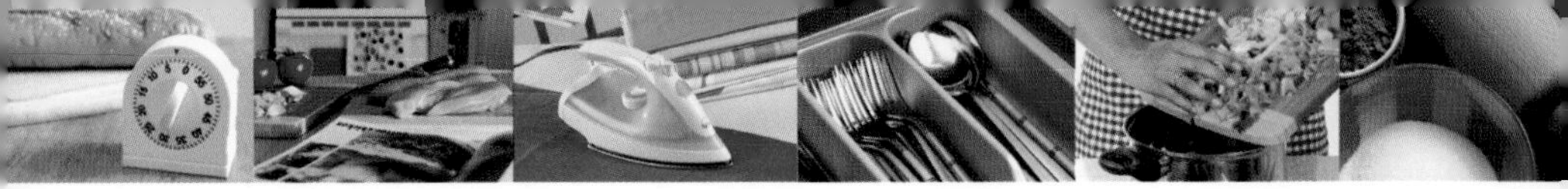

CHAPTER 3

Time-Savers

Claire takes classes in the morning and works at a part-time job in the afternoon. When she gets home, she has to get dinner ready for her family.

But Claire doesn't get stressed about fixing dinner. Even though her time is limited, she knows she can do it.

Over the years, Claire has learned the importance of planning ahead. She's also learned some useful time-savers.

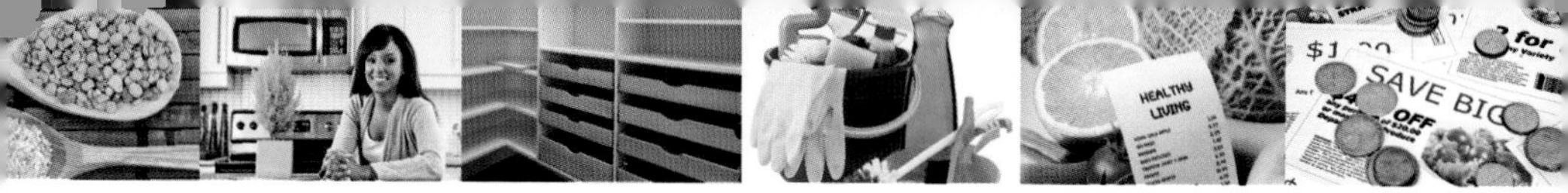

Ingredients to Have on Hand

Having a well-stocked pantry and freezer is important for any home cook. And some of the most useful ingredients to have on hand are canned and frozen vegetables.

Not only are these vegetables cheaper than fresh produce. But they're also easier to prepare. For example, a can of corn or green beans makes a quick and easy side dish. And frozen and canned vegetables are great additions to soups and stews.

Canned and frozen vegetables don't have all of the nutritional benefits of fresh produce. But because they're so easy to prepare, you may serve vegetables more often.

Cooking in Bulk

On Saturday, Claire spent the afternoon cooking in ***bulk***. She made a big pot of spaghetti sauce. She also made some fish stew and a tuna-noodle casserole. Then, she divided everything into meal-size ***portions*** and stored them in the freezer.

Bulk

In a large quantity or size.

Portion

A part or section. When used to describe food, a *portion* is usually a single serving.

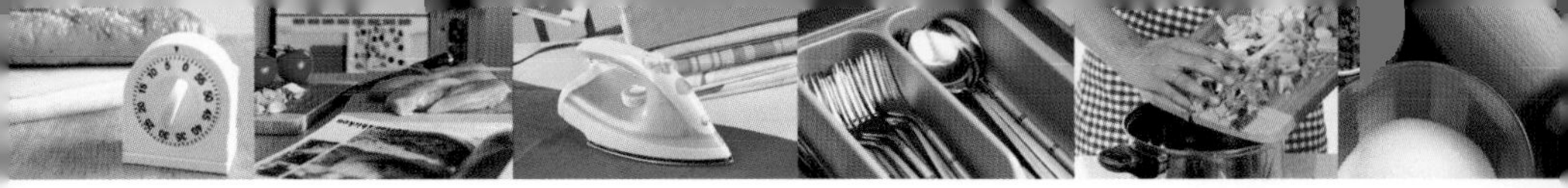

At the end of the day, Claire had enough spaghetti sauce for about 16 servings. She had the same number of servings of stew and casserole.

Over the next few weeks, when she's ready to prepare a meal, she'll thaw out what she needs. Then she'll heat it up on the stove or using the microwave.

Cooking in bulk also saves clean-up time. When Claire fixes dinner this way, she usually has just one or two pots to clean.

Using a Slow Cooker

Sometimes, Claire fixes dinner using a slow cooker. (Her mother calls it a "crock pot.") One of her favorite meals to make is chicken stew.

In the morning, Claire puts chicken, vegetables, and water in the slow cooker. She also adds a few spices for flavor. Then, she turns on the cooker.

The stew cooks slowly all day while Claire is at school and work. It's hot and ready to serve by dinnertime. And the only clean-up is to wash out the cooker.

Using a Microwave

Claire's family likes baked potatoes, but these potatoes take a long time to make! In a regular oven, a large potato can take up to an hour to cook all the way through.

To make baked potatoes in a hurry, Claire cooks them in a microwave oven. This cuts down the baking time by 40 minutes or more. The ***texture*** of microwaved potatoes is different from that of potatoes baked in a regular oven. Micro-waved potatoes aren't quite as soft. But Claire's family doesn't mind.

On busy days, Claire also uses the microwave to cook vegetables. She puts cut-up vegetables in a bowl and adds a little water. Then she covers the bowl and places it in the microwave. After cooking for about 5 minutes on "High," the vegetables are done. All Claire has to do is drain and season the cooked vegetables.

Using the microwave saves not only time but energy. And again, cleaning up is quick and easy.

Texture

The look or feel of something, especially on the surface.

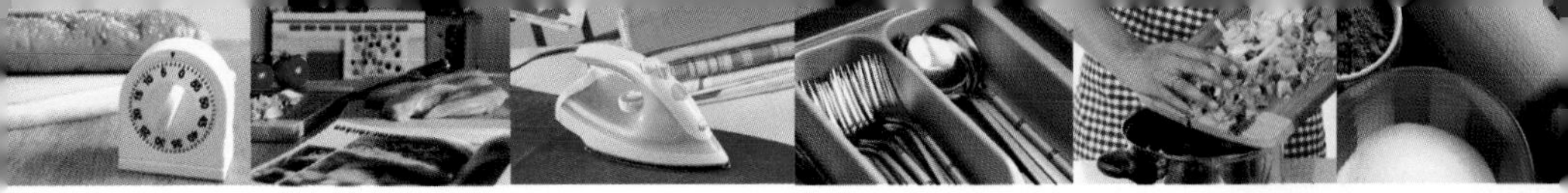

Microwave Safety Tips

- Remove all the packaging when defrosting food in a microwave.
- Cook food immediately after defrosting it, especially meat.
- Don't cook large cuts of meat or whole poultry on "High." (They may explode.)
- Stir or turn food halfway through cooking. This allows it to cook evenly and all the way through.
- Use containers that are labeled "Microwave safe."
- Don't use plastic storage containers to defrost or heat food. (The plastic may melt or warp.)
- Don't allow plastic wrap to touch food while heating it. (The wrap may melt.)
- Don't use plastic storage bags, brown paper or plastic grocery bags, newspaper, or aluminum foil in a microwave. (They may melt or burn.)
- Never put metal containers or utensils in a microwave.

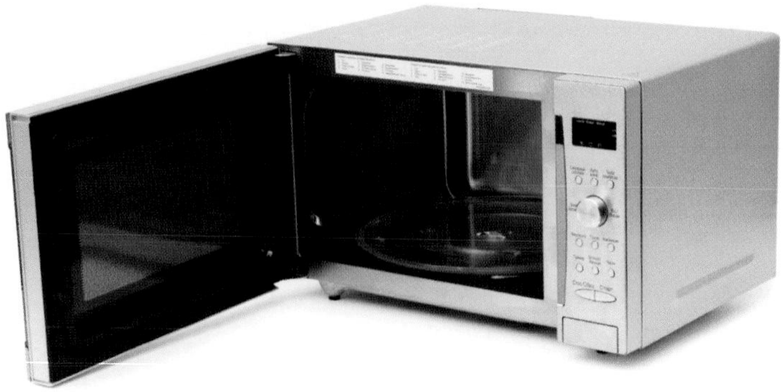

Using a Food Processor

Claire spends very little time chopping vegetables. She uses her food processor to chop, slice, grate, and mince them for her. In addition, the food processor mixes, grinds, and blends. Claire has even used it to make bread and pie dough.

Using Nonstick Pots and Pans

Another time-saver is to use nonstick pots and pans. The nonstick finish prevents foods from sticking to the pots and pans. That makes them much easier to clean.

Tips for a Quick Clean-Up

1. **Plan ahead**. Plan for the clean-up along with the meal. Something as simple as making room in the refrigerator before the meal can save time later when you clean up.
2. **Clean as you cook**. Fill the sink with warm, soapy water. Wash dishes and utensils as you use them. Soak large dishes in the sink to open up room in the dishwasher.
3. **Keep counters and other surfaces clean**. Wipe down counters after you use them to prevent a messy build-up. Likewise, wipe up spills on the stove and in the microwave immediately after they happen.
4. **Use a scrap bowl**. Keep a bowl on your counter near the sink. Throw scraps into it as you clean and cut up vegetables, fruits, and so on. Empty the bowl into the trash after you've finished.

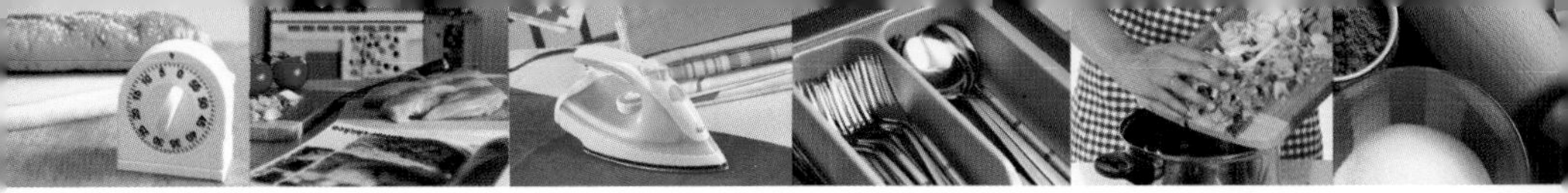

CHAPTER **4**

Following a Recipe

Get Out the Ingredients

Most recipes begin with a list of ingredients. So before you start cooking, make sure you have everything you need.

In a Pinch: Common Ingredient Substitutions

Even the most well organized cook can run out of an important ingredient! Use this chart to know what other ingredients you can use to replace something you don't have.

Ingredient	Amount	Substitution
Baking powder	1 teaspoon	¼ teaspoon baking soda plus ½ teaspoon cream of tartar or ¼ teaspoon baking soda plus ½ cup buttermilk
Bread crumbs	1 cup	1 cup cracker crumbs or 1 cup ground oats

Ingredient	Amount	Substitution
Broth (beef or chicken)	1 cup	1 bouillon cube plus 1 cup boiling water or 1 cup vegetable broth
Brown sugar	1 cup, packed	1 cup white sugar plus ¼ cup molasses and decrease the liquid in recipe by ¼ cup or 1 cup white sugar
Butter	1 cup	1 cup margarine or 1 cup shortening plus ½ teaspoon salt
Chocolate (semisweet)	1 ounce	1 (1-ounce) square of unsweetened chocolate plus 4 teaspoons sugar or 1 ounce semisweet chocolate chips plus 1 teaspoon shortening
Cocoa	¼ cup	1 (1-ounce) square unsweetened chocolate
Cream	1 cup	1 cup evaporated milk or ¾ cup milk plus 1/3 cup butter
Egg	1 whole	¼ cup liquid egg substitute or half a banana mashed with ½ teaspoon baking powder
Garlic	1 clove	⅛ teaspoon garlic powder
Herbs (fresh)	1 tablespoon chopped fresh	1 teaspoon (chopped or whole leaf) dried herbs
Ketchup	1 cup	1 cup tomato sauce plus 1 teaspoon vinegar plus 1 tablespoon sugar
Mayonnaise	1 cup	1 cup sour cream or 1 cup plain yogurt
Stock	1 cup	1 cube beef or chicken bouillon in 1 cup water
Vegetable oil	1 cup	1 cup applesauce
Vinegar	1 teaspoon	1 teaspoon lemon or lime juice or 2 teaspoons white wine
White sugar	1 cup	1 cup brown sugar or 1¼ cups confectioners' (powdered) sugar or ¾ cup honey
Yogurt	1 cup	1 cup sour cream or 1 cup buttermilk

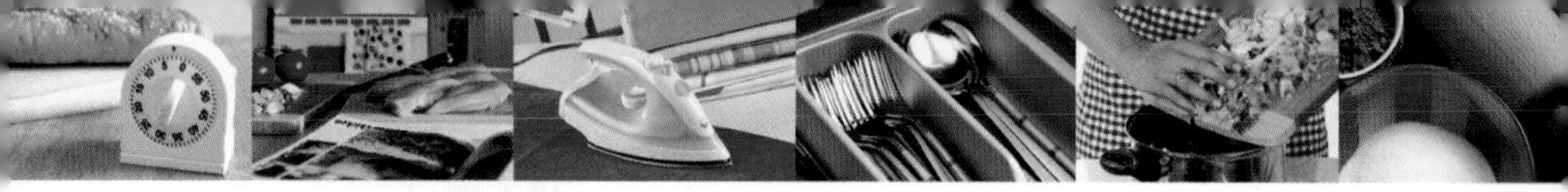

Get out all the ingredients, and put them on the counter. That way, you can follow the steps in the recipe without stopping to look for something.

Spices to Keep in the Cabinet

With a well-stocked spice cabinet, you can liven up any dish and make it uniquely your own. Here are a few spices you should always have on hand:

- **Salt and black ground pepper:** Salt and pepper are the two most common seasonings in everyday cooking.
- **Garlic powder:** Garlic is another popular seasoning. Garlic powder can also be used as a substitute for salt.
- **Cajun seasoning:** This spice is a combination of several spices. Its flavor is often described as both smoky and spicy. Cajun seasoning can be used to spice up a wide range of foods.
- **Crushed red pepper flakes:** Red pepper flakes add hot flavor to foods. They are also believed to help increase the body's metabolism.
- **Ground cumin:** Cumin has a strong, smoky flavor. It's commonly used in Latin American cooking. It's also used in chili and barbeque sauce, plus other sauces and dips.
- **Cinnamon:** Both sweet and savory foods often contain cinnamon. This spice is also believed to have many health benefits.

Learn the Vocabulary

Cooking has a language all its own. To understand a recipe, you need to understand the special ***vocabulary*** of cooking.

The following lists contain some words you're likely to see in a cookbook. Did you know there were so many ways to cut and cook food?

> **Vocabulary**
> The set of words or terms used in a specific subject area.
>
> **Irregular**
> Uneven or unequal.

Cutting Methods

Cube: Cut the food into $\frac{1}{2}$-inch strips. Line up the strips. Then cut crosswise to form cubes.

Dice: Cut the food into $\frac{1}{4}$-inch strips. Line up and stack the strips. Then cut crosswise to form small pieces.

Chop: Cut the food into ***irregular***, pea-size pieces.

Finely chop: Cut the food into pieces smaller than peas.

Slice and bias-slice: To slice, cut food crosswise. To bias-slice, cut holding the knife at a 45-degree angle to the cutting surface.

Julienne: Cut the food into strips $\frac{1}{2}$ inch thick and 2 inches long. Stack the slices. Then cut lengthwise again to make thin, match-like strips.

Shred: Move the food across a shredding surface to make long, narrow strips.

Finely shred: Move the food across a fine-shredding surface to make small, thin strips.

Mince: Cut food into tiny, irregularly shaped pieces.

Grate: Rub the food across a grating surface to make fine pieces.

Cooking Methods

Simmer: Heat a liquid over low heat until bubbles form and begin to burst below the surface.

Boil: Heat a liquid over high heat until bubbles form and rise steadily, breaking on the surface.

Poach: Cook food partly or completely by ***submerging*** it in simmering liquid.

Steam: Cook food in the steam given off by boiling water. Place the food in a metal basket, a bamboo steamer, or a rack set above the water. Cover the pot and steam until the food is done.

Stir-fry: Cook food quickly over high heat in a lightly oiled wok or skillet. Lift and turn the food constantly.

Deep-fat fry: Submerge food in hot, melted shortening or cooking oil. Stir food and remove it when it's golden brown and crisp.

Bake: Cook food in the indirect, dry heat of an oven. The food may be covered or uncovered.

Broil: Cook food a measured distance from the direct, dry heat of the heat source.

Grill: Cook food on a wire grid above a dry heat source, such as propane gas, wood, or charcoal.

Submerge

To plunge under water or another liquid.

Avoiding Kitchen Injuries

Many people get hurt while cooking and cleaning up. Common injuries include cuts, burns, falls, eye injuries, and reactions to spices and chemicals.

To avoid getting hurt, follow these guidelines:

- Keep your workspace clean and organized.
- Keep your knives sharp, and store them properly.
- When using a knife, always make cuts away from your body.
- When holding the food you're cutting, curl up your fingers into your hand.
- Use utensils, not your fingers, to move foods in and out of hot liquids.
- Don't touch your face (especially your eyes) while chopping peppers or other spicy foods.
- Keep floors clean by mopping up spills immediately.
- Don't overload electrical outlets.
- Keep potholders and oven mitts near the stove and oven, so you'll be sure to use them.
- Keep a well-stocked first-aid kit in a kitchen cabinet.

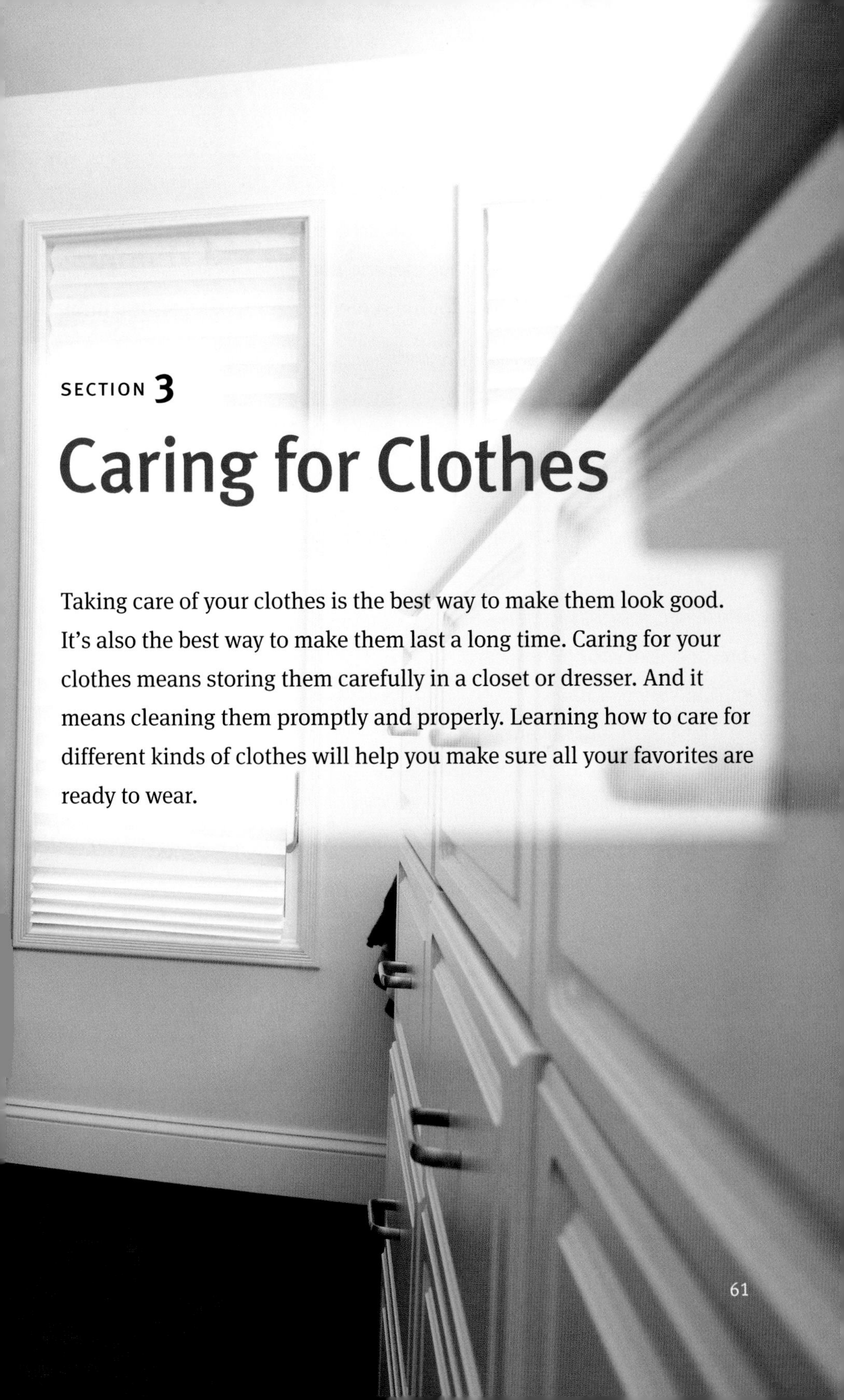

SECTION 3

Caring for Clothes

Taking care of your clothes is the best way to make them look good. It's also the best way to make them last a long time. Caring for your clothes means storing them carefully in a closet or dresser. And it means cleaning them promptly and properly. Learning how to care for different kinds of clothes will help you make sure all your favorites are ready to wear.

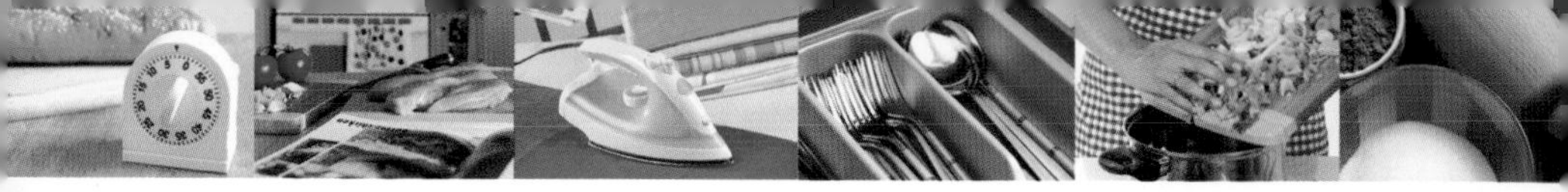

Learning Some Hard Lessons

Justin had never paid much attention to doing the laundry. When he lived with his family, his mother had tried repeatedly to teach him. "You'll need to know how to do this someday," Mom kept telling him.

Justin's dad had also tried to get him to take care of his clothes. Dad made a weekly trip to the dry cleaner to have his shirts washed and ironed. He also had his suits cleaned every couple of weeks. Using these services was expensive but necessary for taking care of Dad's nice clothes.

But Justin had never been interested in any of this. All he'd cared about was that he found clean clothes in the dresser when he opened the drawer.

Now, Justin wished he'd paid attention. After living on his own for a few months, he'd ruined a lot of clothes trying to care for them.

In fact, Justin's first load of laundry was a disaster! He'd put a new red sweatshirt in with his light-colored socks, T-shirts, and underwear. Washing the load in hot water had turned all the light-colored clothes pink. And the

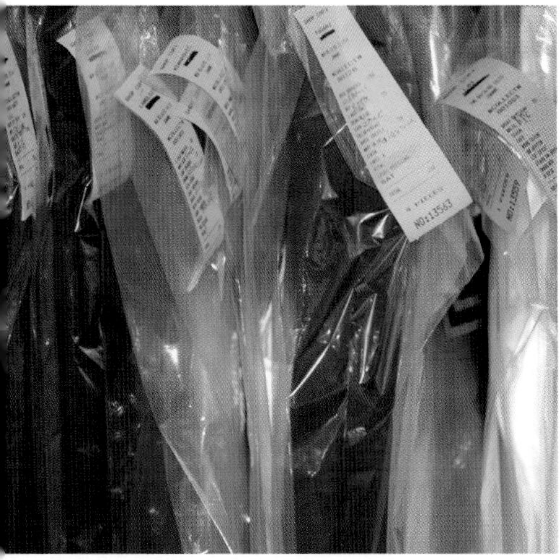

sweatshirt had shrunk at least a size too small.

Justin had also ruined some clothes trying to iron them. When he tried to press a shirt, he got the iron too hot and made a burn mark on the collar.

Later, Justin tried to press a pair of dress pants. Doing that would be faster and cheaper than having them dry-cleaned, he thought. But pressing a crease down the leg made a dark stain. The pants were dirty, Justin realized. And now, they were ruined!

CHAPTER **1**

Organizing a Closet and Dresser

Being kind to your clothes will keep them in good shape. That includes storing them properly in a closet or dresser.

Organizing your closet and dresser will help make sure your clothes are clean and wrinkle free when you want to wear them. Organizing your clothes will also help you ***simplify*** dressing.

Simplify

To make easier or faster.

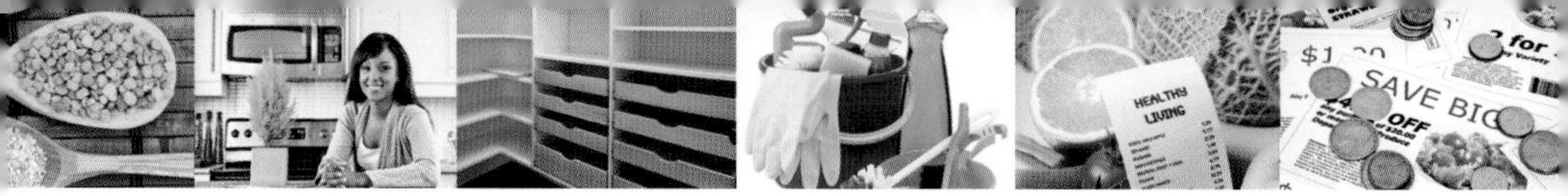

Tips for Organizing Your Closet

- To keep shirts and dresses hanging straight, button all the top buttons.
- Keep together clothes from different categories—all shirts, all pants, and so on.
- Don't hang knit clothes unless they're woven very tightly and you wear them often. If you do hang a knit item, fold it once the long way. Then hang it over the bar on the hanger. For extra care, put crisp white tissue paper in the fold to prevent creasing.
- Once in a while, leave the closet door slightly open to let the air ***circulate.*** This will keep your closet fresh.
- Hang small packets of ***fragrant*** herbs in the closet to keep your clothes smelling good.

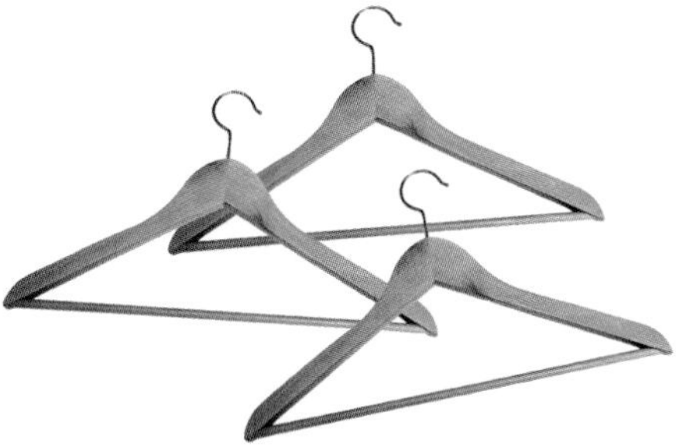

Circulate

To flow through.

Fragrant

Sweet or pleasant smelling.

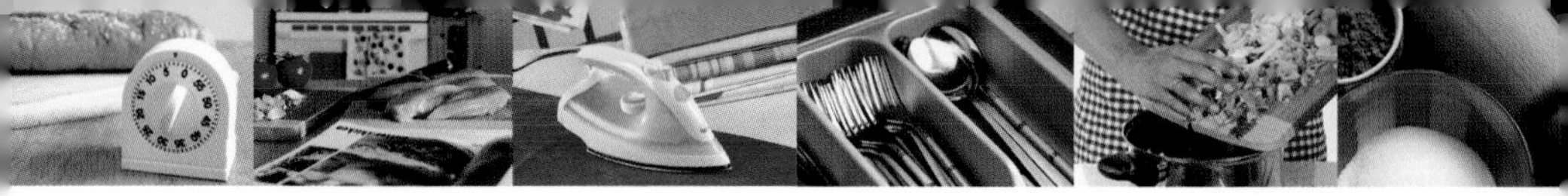

How to Clean Your Closet

1. To prepare, get three boxes. Label them "Trash," "Out of Place," and "Donate." Also buy several stackable bins.
2. Pick one section of the closet to work on—maybe a shelf or the floor.
3. Take everything out of the section.
4. Look at each item. Ask yourself if you've used it in the past year. If not, put it in the "Trash" or "Donate" box.
5. Place each item that belongs somewhere else in the "Out of Place" box. Find the proper place for it later.
6. Sort the items you want to keep:
   - Hang the items that belong on hangers.
   - Put shoes and other items on shelves or in racks, if possible.
   - Place the remaining items in labeled bins—maybe "Purses" or "Softball Gear."
7. Arrange the labeled bins so it's easiest to reach the ones you use most often.
8. Repeat this process with each section of your closet.

Tools for Organizing for Your Closet

Like many jobs, organizing your closet will be easier if you have the right tools.

Hangers

- Keep extra hangers in your closet, so one is always available when you need it.
- Use padded hangers for knits and wooden hangers for coats and jackets.

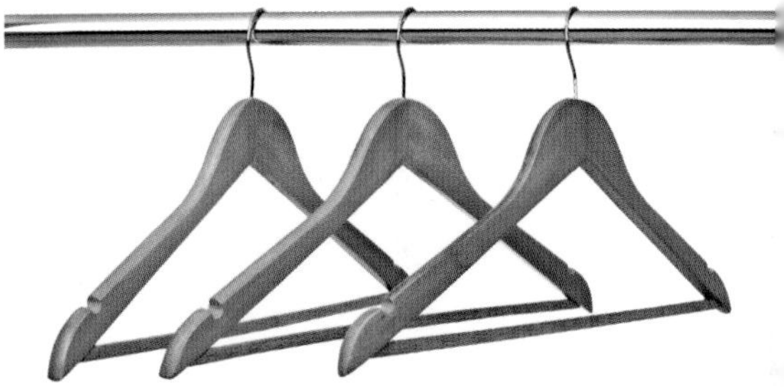

- Avoid crushing your clothes by spacing hangers as far apart as possible. Using padded and wooden hangers will make this easier.

Hanging Bags, Racks, and Shelves

- Use hanging racks and shelves to store shoes. Doing so will make it easier to keep the floor of the closet clean. (Keeping the floor clean will ***discourage*** pests such as moths and carpet beetles, which can ruin clothes.)
- Also use hanging shelves for sweaters and other knit items you don't want to hang.

Discourage

To try to stop or convince not to do.

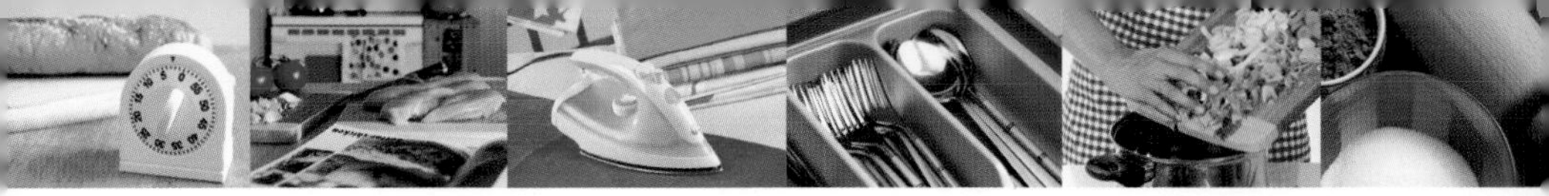

→ Store clothes from different seasons in hanging bags to protect them from dust.

Never hang an item of clothing on a hook or a doorknob unless it has a loop in the collar for hanging and it doesn't need to be ironed. Your bathrobe can be hung up this way!

Tips for Organizing Your Dresser

→ Line dresser drawers with good shelf paper or drawer liners. Doing so will prevent damage to the clothing from acid or splinters in the wood.

→ Some liners have a pleasant scent. But avoid gummed or prepasted paper, because the glue attracts some insects.

- If possible, store clothes in many shallow drawers rather than a few deep ones. Tightly packed clothes get wrinkled and are hard to find.
- If you have to stack clothes in drawers, put lighter items on top of heavier items.
- Put knits and clothes made of soft fabrics in the dresser, not the closet. Hanging them will make them lose their shape.
- Before putting an item of clothing in a drawer, press it out flat. Then either roll or fold the item neatly.
- If you fold clothes, try to put the folds where they won't show when the clothes are worn. For example, fold along the seams or on the waistband.

Problems with Scented Products

Scented air fresheners, shelf papers, and other products will make your closet or dresser smell good. But over time, they can cause health problems. The scents get into your clothes, and you carry them to work or school.

Some people develop serious reactions to the chemicals in these products. The symptoms include runny nose, watery eyes, trouble breathing, headache, nausea, dizziness, and fatigue.

Because of health issues with scents, some workplaces have a no-fragrance policy.

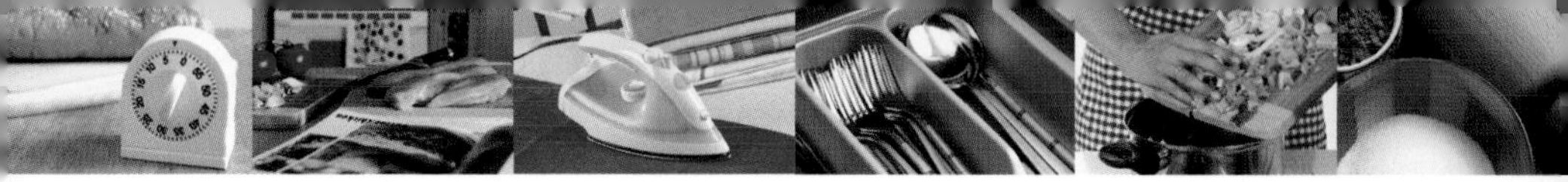

CHAPTER **2**

Doing the Laundry

How you take care of your clothes is important. Clothes last longer when they're well taken care of.

Taking care of your clothes is also important to your appearance. After all, your clothing makes a ***statement*** about you.

For both these reasons, you need to learn how to do laundry correctly.

Follow the Rules!

Doing laundry isn't hard! Following three simple rules will keep your whites white and your colors bright.

Statement

A factual report or announcement.

Rule 1: Sort your laundry before you load it into the washing machine.

- Wash colored clothing with other colored clothing of the same darkness or brightness. In other words, wash lights in one load, brights in another, and darks in another.
- Wash whites *only* with other whites. To qualify for the "white" load, the item of clothing must have no color on it at all. Other colors can fade or bleed onto your whites. This means that a sock with a red stripe around the top does *not* go in with the whites.
- Also sort clothes according to how dirty they are. Wash very dirty clothes in their own load. Before washing extremely dirty clothes, soak them in soapy water and then rinse them.

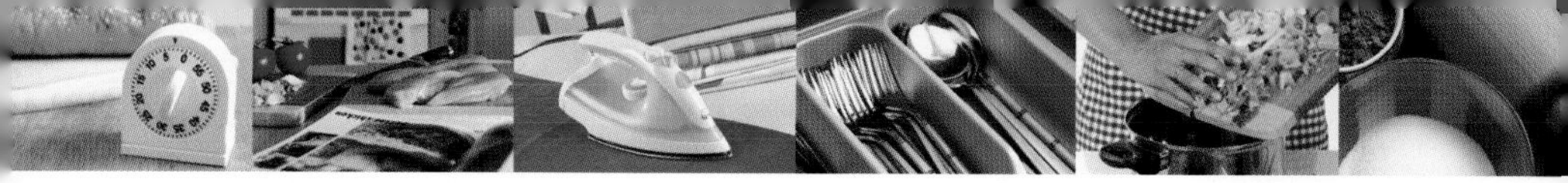

Tips for Clothing Care

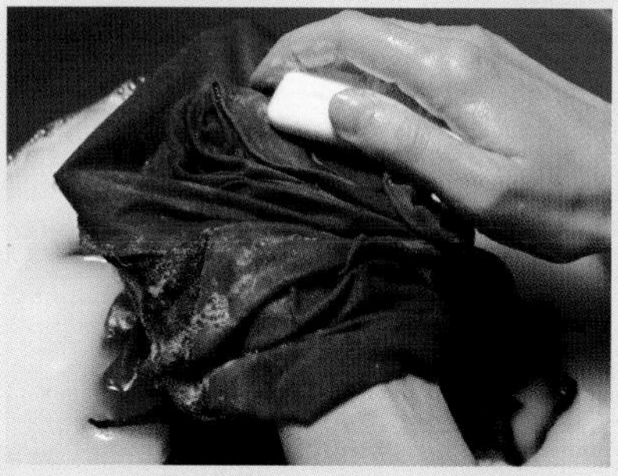

- Wash clothes only when they're dirty. If clothes are only wrinkled, not dirty, then iron them.
- Iron clothes only when they're wrinkled. But don't iron dirty clothes!
- Air-dry clothes as much as possible. Hang them or lay them flat.
- Follow the care instructions on clothing labels.
- Fix rips, tears, and loose buttons as soon as possible. Don't wash clothes until after they've been mended.
- Treat stains as soon as possible with stain or spot remover. Then wash them immediately in cold water. Repeat if necessary.

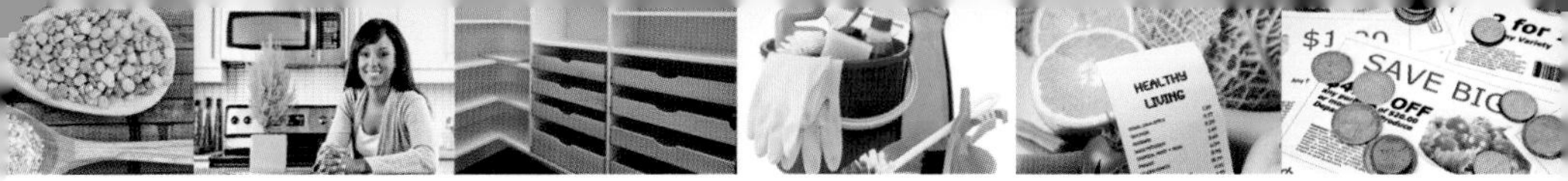

Rule 2: Deal with stains before you do the laundry.

Heat makes stains ***permanent.*** So, washing something in hot water and drying it in a hot dryer can make it impossible to remove a stain.

> **Permanent**
>
> Unable to be changed.

For best results, treat stains as soon as possible. Fresh stains are much easier to remove than old stains.

Follow these additional tips:

- If you don't have a stain remover, make a paste by mixing powdered laundry detergent with a little water. Then, rub the paste into the stain. Or rub a little liquid detergent into the stain.
- Lightly scrub the stain using a small brush, like a fingernail brush or an old toothbrush. Then launder the clothing as usual.

Rule 3: Use the proper heat settings.

Using the wrong water temperature can ruin your clothing, too. Clothes can shrink, colors can bleed, and white items can turn gray!

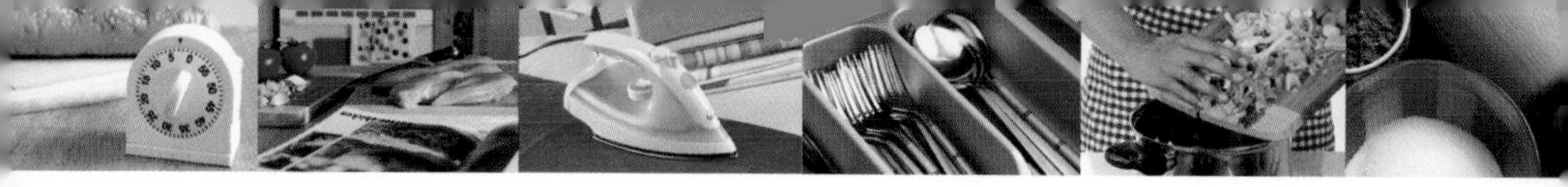

Follow these guidelines for heat settings:

- **Whites:** Hot water wash, cold rinse
- **Wash-and-wear colored fabrics:** Warm water wash, cold rinse
- ***Elastic* fabrics:** Warm water wash, cold rinse
- ***Synthetic* fabrics:** Warm water wash, cold rinse
- **Colored fabrics that bleed:** Cool water wash, cold rinse
- **Woolens:** Cool water wash, cold rinse

Elastic

Stretchy. Elastic fabrics are used to make clothing such as T-shirts, sweatshirts, and most sportswear.

Synthetic

Made by a chemical process. Not occurring naturally. Synthetic fabrics include polyester, nylon, lycra, and rayon.

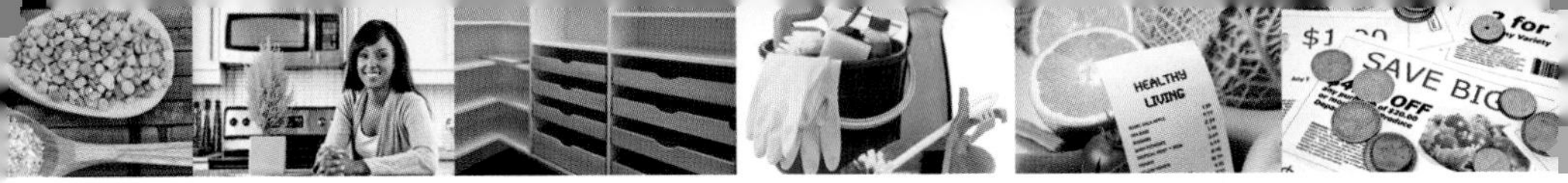

Tips for Treating Stains

General Stain Treatment

- Dab at the stain using a sponge wetted with lukewarm water.
- For whites, follow up with bleach, if necessary.
- Don't dry the item in the dryer until the stain has been completely removed.

Specific Types of Stains

- **Fruit, juice, wine, rust, or tea:** Stretch the fabric over a bowl or sink. Then pour boiling water through the stain.
- **Blood or ink:** Using cold water, soak the stained item. Then wash and rinse.
- **Chocolate or coffee:** Sponge the stain with cold water. Then mix two tablespoons of Borax or other detergent in warm water, and sponge the stain again.
- **Grass or mildew:** Wash the item in hot, soapy water. Rinse and air-dry.
- **Gravy:** Wash or sponge the item with lukewarm, soapy water.
- **Grease, oil, or lipstick:** Using very hot water, wash with liquid detergent.
- **Perspiration:** Sponge with a mix of white vinegar and water.

CHAPTER 3

Information on Clothing Labels

Some clothes should be washed only in cold water. Others should be washed in water that's warm or hot. Rinsing in cold water is fine for nearly all kinds of clothes, and it ***conserves*** energy, too.

How do you know if you're using the right temperatures for your clothes? The best way to find out is to check the care labels. You can find the care label on an item of clothing inside the collar, inside the waistband, or on one of the inside side seams.

Conserve

To save or protect.

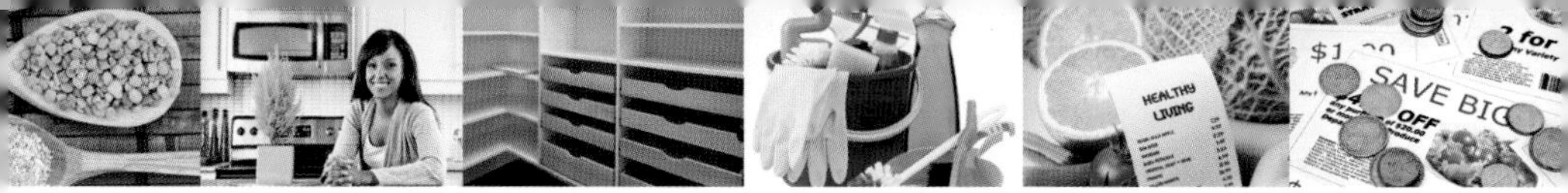

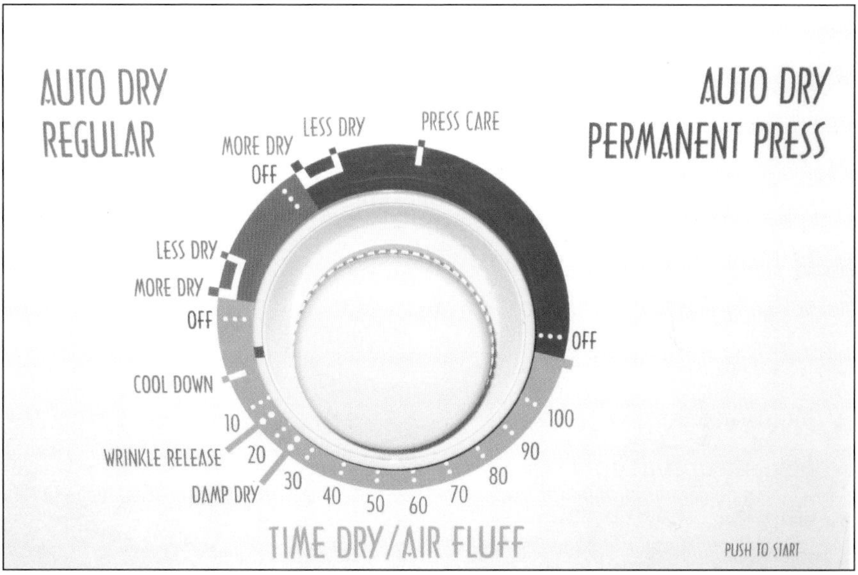

Labeling Requirements

By law in the United States, all clothing must have care labels. The only exceptions are shoes, caps, hats, and gloves.

Care labels must do the following:

- List washing or dry-cleaning instructions.
- Be easily readable before the item is purchased.
- Be permanent for the life of the garment.
- Tell if any part of the regular care of the item could be harmful.

- Warn that a garment can't be cleaned by a certain method.
- List the ***appropriate*** water temperature, if hot water will harm the item.
- List the appropriate dryer setting, if hot air will harm the item.
- List the recommended iron setting, if using a hot iron will harm the item.
- Mention that bleach is not safe or that only non-chlorine bleach is safe.

Appropriate
Proper or acceptable.

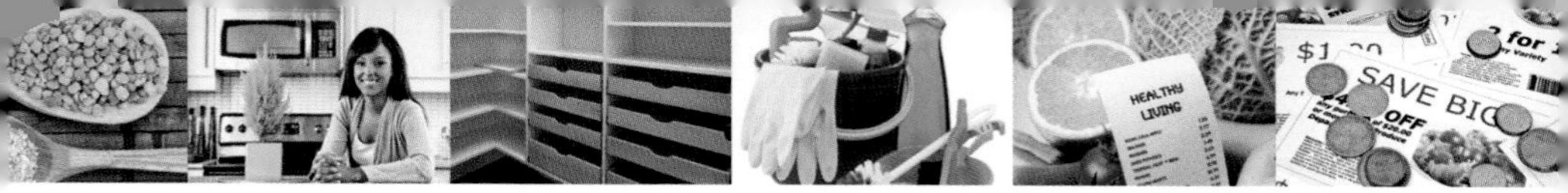

Reading the Label

See the example at the right to get an idea of what a care label looks like.

Also learn the meanings of these terms to understand what the label is telling you to do.

Term	Meaning
Hot water	Use water up to 150°.
Warm water	Use water between 90° and 110°.
Cold water	Use water up to 85°.
Durable or permanent press cycle	Cool rinse before spinning to reduce wrinkling.
With like colors	Wash with clothing of similar color and brightness.
Dry flat	Lay out horizontally to dry.
Block to dry	Reshape to original ***dimensions*** before allowing the clothing to air-dry.
Only non-chlorine bleach, when needed	Chlorine bleach may damage the clothing.

You can also find clothing care information online at Web sites such as www.textileaffairs.com/lguide.htm.

Durable

Sturdy and long lasting.

Dimensions

Measurements, such as length and width.

[FACT]

Clothing Label Requirements

The Federal Trade Commission (FTC) is the part of the US government that oversees clothing labels. The FTC works with clothing manufacturers to make sure two kinds of labels are provided:

1. **Care labels** provide instructions for washing and drying. They also note anything that could harm an item, such as ironing or machine washing.
2. **Content labels** say what the fabric is made of, the country it came from, and what company made the product or brought it to the United States.

COTTON
MADE IN CHINA
SEE BACK FOR CARE

CARE:
MACHINE WASH WARM
WASH WITH LIKE COLORS
ONLY NON-CHLORINE
BLEACH WHEN NEEDED
TUMBLE DRY LOW
WARM IRON IF NEEDED

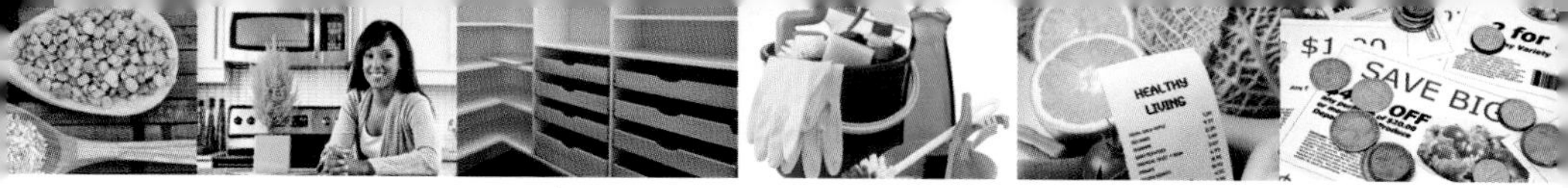

How to Dry Clothes Flat

Care labels that specify air drying also sometimes say to "dry flat." Doing so prevents the extra water weight from stretching knitted garments, such as sweaters.

To dry a clothing item flat, follow these steps:

1. **Prepare a space.** Lay a towel on a table, or buy and set up a flat drying rack.
2. **Place the garment.** Lay the item on the towel or rack. Carefully arrange it in its proper shape. Check pockets, collars, and necklines, too.
3. **Let it dry.** Drying will usually take a day or more, depending on how thick the fabric is. When the top of the item is dry, turn it over to speed up drying.

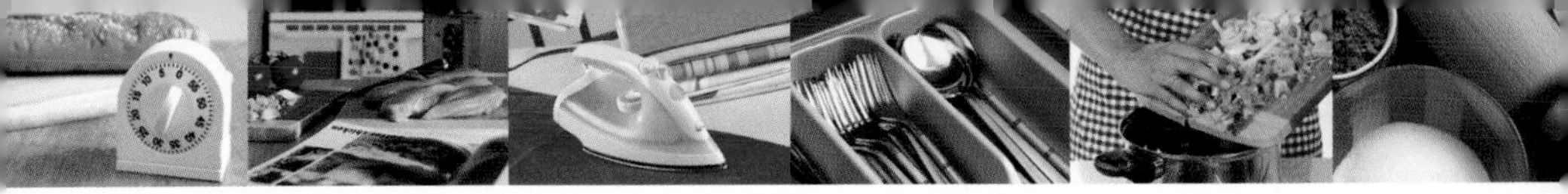

CHAPTER 4

Ironing, Dry Cleaning, and Storing Clothes

Tips for Ironing

→ Most fabrics are easier to iron if they are *damp*, or slightly wet. To make sure clothes are damp, take them out of the dryer before they're completely dry. You can also spray them with a water bottle. Or you can use a steam iron to dampen the clothes as you iron.

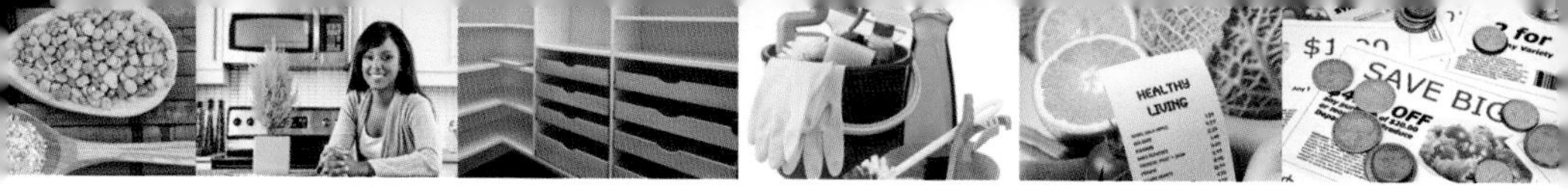

- Use spray starch to dampen tailored shirts and other items you want to look crisp. Spray the starch lightly and evenly across the item. You can buy spray starch or make your own: Mix one tablespoon cornstarch into two cups of water, and pour it into spray bottle.

- Check the heat setting on the iron. Choose the setting that's appropriate for the fabric. If the setting is too hot, you'll likely ruin synthetics and blends.

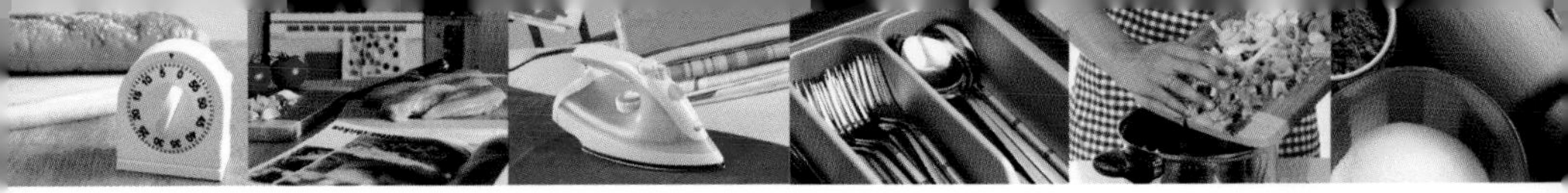

Ironing Tips

- Check the iron setting, and make sure it's correct before touching the iron to the clothing.
- Iron those items with "High" heat settings first. Then each time you lower the setting, give the iron a minute or two to cool down.
- Iron collars, cuffs, and hems on the wrong side first to prevent puckering. Then turn over and iron on the right side.
- Insert a rolled-up towel inside a sleeve or pant leg to prevent forming creases.
- Iron wash-and-wear fabrics inside out to avoid making them shiny. Or cover them with a cotton dishtowel or pillow cloth before ironing on the right side.
- Prevent creating new wrinkles by moving freshly ironed areas away from you.

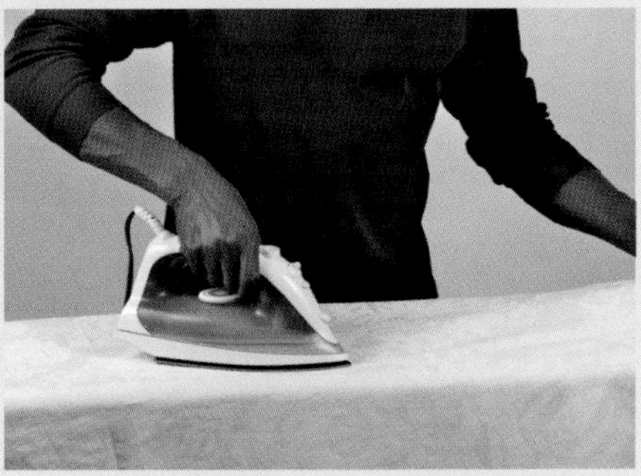

Tips for Dry Cleaning

→ Dry-clean clothes as little as possible. Why? The dry-cleaning process is hard on them. Clothing that's only wrinkled may not need dry cleaning. At your request, most cleaners will press a garment without cleaning it. ***Infrequent*** dry cleaning is easier on your budget *and* your clothes.

- Don't have something pressed that's even slightly dirty. The heat involved in pressing may make a nearly ***invisible*** stain turn brown or set it permanently.
- During the dry-cleaning process, ***subtle*** color changes can take place in clothing. So always make sure to dry-clean *both* parts of a two-piece outfit at the same time. This is true even if only the jacket of a suit needs cleaning. Otherwise, you might end up with a suit jacket that's a slightly lighter color than the pants or skirt.

Infrequent
Not happening often or regularly.

Invisible
Impossible to see.

Subtle
Slight or not obvious.

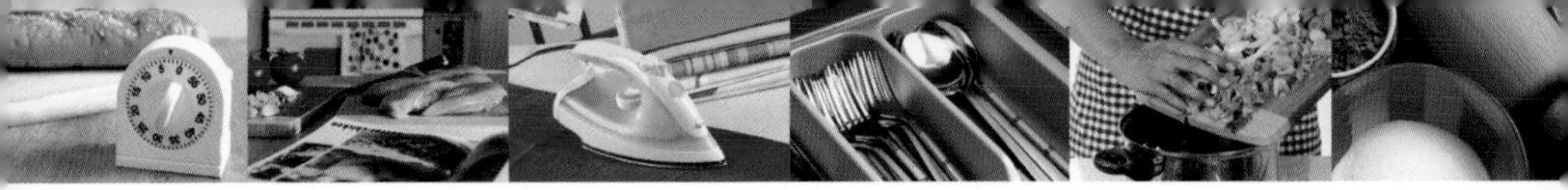

How Does Dry Cleaning Work?

1. **Tagging and pretreating:** An identification tag is pinned on each garment. Then any stains are pretreated.
2. **Washing:** Clothes are put in a machine like a large washing machine. A liquid chemical called *perchlorethyline*, or *perc*, is pumped through the machine as it spins. (The process is called *dry cleaning* because no water is used.)
3. **Rinsing:** A drain cycle spins the clothes to remove the perc.
4. **Drying:** Warm air blows through the machine.
5. **Inspection:** The person operating the machine looks for any remaining spots and treats them.
6. **Pressing:** A pressing machine uses steam and pressure to straighten the garments. Then it vacuums out the steam, leaving the clothes dry.

Tips for Storing

- Never store dirty clothes. Over time, dirt and stains will become much more difficult to remove. And some types of stains may attract bugs.

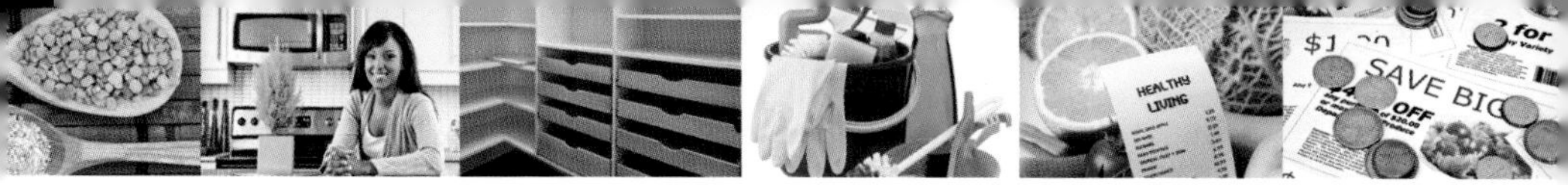

- Before storing clothes, be certain that all ***traces*** of detergent have been removed. Even tiny traces can cause chemical changes over time.

> **Traces**
> Small amounts that have been left behind.

- Don't store items that have been starched. Starch attracts insects called *silverfish*.
- Store clothes in clean plastic bins or boxes, a clean suitcase, or even unused drawers in an extra dresser. Store hanging clothes in a hanging bag (preferably with shelves) in a closet.

- Covering clothes will help to keep out water, dust, mold, bacteria, and smoke. Use muslin bags or cover clothing with sheets. Avoid using plastic bags for some clothes or for long periods of time, because they cut off air. Without air, leather and suede will dry out, and fabrics will slowly break down. And moisture trapped in bags can form mildew and leave stains.

SECTION 4

Home Maintenance and Decorating

Your home would always be spotless if you had a live-in cleaning person. And it would be decorated exactly how you'd like it if you hired an interior designer. But chances are, you can't afford to hire people to perform these services. That means you need to know how to clean and decorate your home yourself. It won't always be fun! But you'll feel satisfied to know that you did it yourself.

Making a New House a Home

Nikki had heard people talk about "fixer-uppers." And now, she knew what that term meant!

Her family had just moved to a small town and bought a new house. Actually, it was an old house—almost 100 years old. But they loved it. It was exactly the kind of house her parents had always dreamed of owning.

The house needed a lot of work, however. To begin, it needed a thorough cleaning. The previous owners hadn't done much housekeeping, it seemed. Everything in the house was covered with dust.

Scrubbing the wood and tile floors got them sparkling clean. But shampooing the carpet did little good. It would have to be torn up and replaced. Not cleaning the carpet for so many years had ruined it.

The kitchen was especially dirty. Cleaning the grease off the oven and stove required some heavy-duty cleaning products. Nikki and her sister worked a whole day to get the kitchen clean.

Nikki was excited to start decorating her bedroom. After repairing some small holes in the walls, she was going to paint the room. She'd already picked out the type and color of paint. She planned on doing the work herself.

Nikki was going to have the same bedroom furniture she'd had in her family's previous house. She also had a big, heavy mirror that she'd need help hanging. Her dad would help her make sure it was mounted securely.

Nikki also had some inexpensive decorating ideas. She'd read about finding interesting paintings, vases, pillows, and rugs at second-hand stores. She'd seen a couple of these stores in town and wanted to find out what they had. Who knew what treasures she'd find?

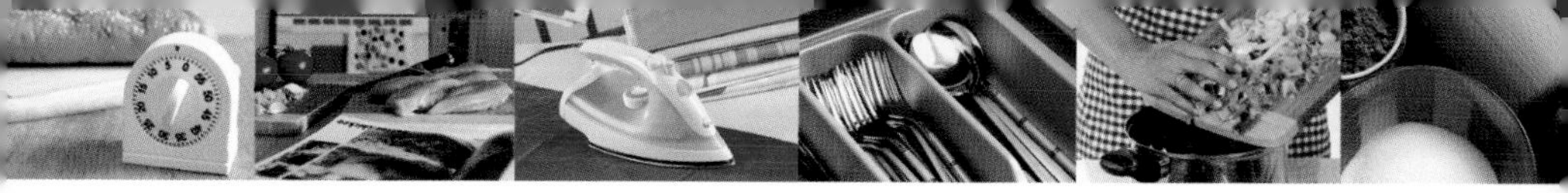

CHAPTER 1

Following a Cleaning Schedule

Eli, Chen, and Justin are roommates in a three-bedroom/one-bath house. They have two cats.

When the roommates moved in together, they agreed they'd rather have a clean house than a messy house. But the more they talked, the more they realized they had two questions.

Basic Cleaning Equipment and Supplies

Cleaning Equipment

- Vacuum
- Broom and dustpan
- Mop and bucket
- Toilet brush and caddy
- Toilet plunger
- Squeegee (for windows and shower)
- Dust cloths and feather duster
- Rags and soft cloths
- Sponges
- Scrub brush
- Rubber gloves

Cleaning Supplies

- All-purpose cleaner
- Disinfectant cleaner
- Window cleaner
- Abrasive cleaner
- Household ammonia
- Automatic dishwasher detergent
- Dish soap
- White vinegar
- Baking soda
- Chlorine bleach
- Spot carpet cleaner
- Laundry detergent

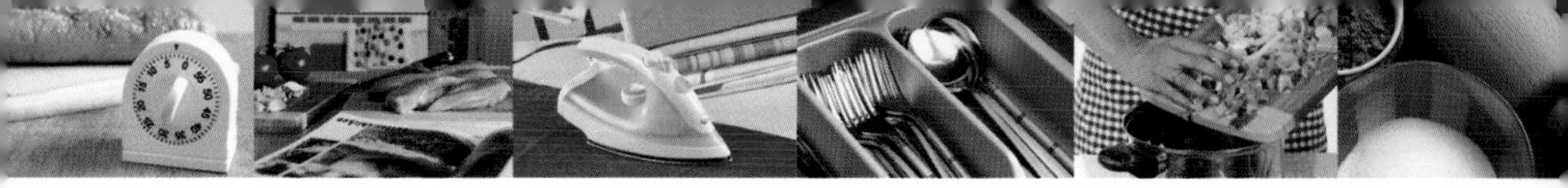

What Needs to Be Done?

None of the roommates had ever had their own house before. All three had lived at home with their families. And even though they'd helped out, they hadn't been responsible for cleaning an entire house.

Housecleaning Tips for Pet Owners

- Use a lint brush to pick up hair or fur from furniture.
- Vacuum or damp-mop floors every day or two to pick up hair or fur.
- Place a large doormat at the main entry to collect the dirt that pets track in. Shake out the mat every couple of days.

- Bathe and groom the pet frequently to limit shedding and odors.
- Provide a towel, rug, blanket, or bed for the pet to lie on. Launder the item regularly. Add vinegar to the wash water to get rid of odors.
- Clean out the litter box daily. Replace the litter weekly, in most cases.
- Clean out the cage and replace bedding material weekly.
- To clean up accidents: Pick up as much material as possible. Soak up wetness with a towel. Spray the area with an enzyme cleaner such as Nature's Miracle or Petastic. Then blot using a clean, damp rag. Using this special kind of cleaner will help get rid of the odor.

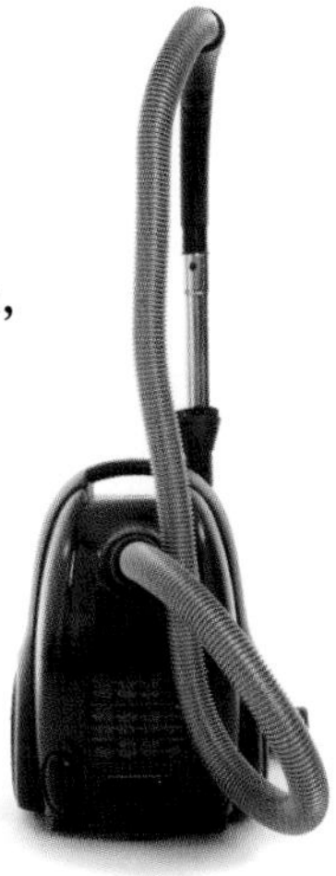

The roommates decided to make a list of jobs. They started with a job they knew about: cleaning their bedrooms. Then they wrote down some jobs they'd done at different times at home: cleaning the bathroom, emptying the garbage, and taking care of pets.

Eli, Chen, and Justin split some jobs into several parts. For instance, some of the kitchen jobs needed to be done on an ***ongoing*** basis. Each roommate should clean up his own mess after using the kitchen. But other jobs needed to be done less often—like washing the floor.

With some help from parents and friends, the roommates came up with a list of jobs. And that led to their second question!

Who's Going to Do the Work?

Of course, no one wanted to be responsible for doing all the work! So, the roommates made a ***schedule*** of jobs that must be done regularly.

The schedule that follows will be in effect for one week. After a week, the roommates will change the names over columns 2, 3, and 4. The week after that, they'll ***rotate*** the jobs by changing the names again.

Ongoing
Constant. Never ending.

Schedule
A plan for when to do one or more activities.

Rotate
To take turns or do in a different order.

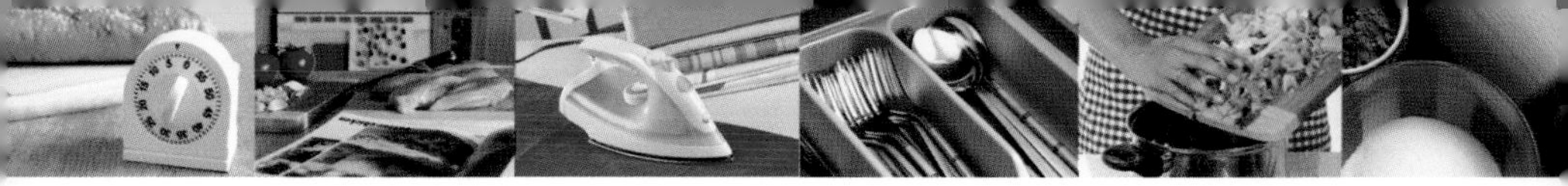

Weekly Cleaning Schedule

Job	Eli	
Empty garbage and take out recycling	Rotate—When full, at least once a week	
Load dishwasher		
Empty dishwasher	Rotate—When necessary	
Clean kitchen counters and sink		
Sweep kitchen floor	Monday, Tuesday	
Wash kitchen floor	Saturday	
Feed cats and clean up after them	Monday, Tuesday	
Clean out cats' litter box	Monday, Tuesday	
Clean toilet and bathroom	Rotate—At least once a week	
Wipe down shower stall		
Vacuum common living areas	Saturday	
Dust common living areas		
Water plants in common living areas		
Make bed		
Clean bedroom: Vacuum, dust, change sheets		
Do laundry		

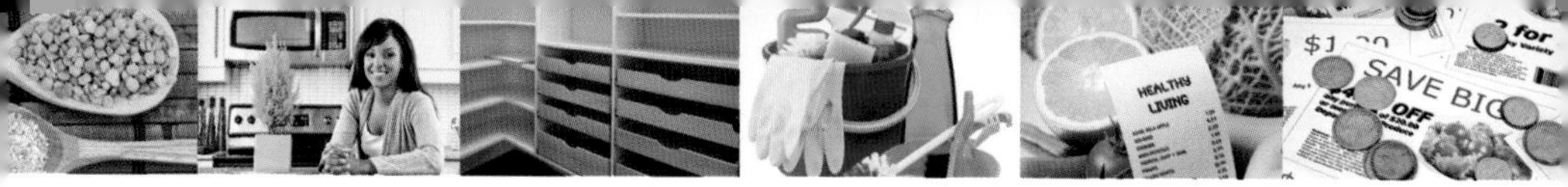

Chen	Justin	Do Your Own
		Daily—Rinse and load your own dishes
		Daily—Clean them as you use them
Wednesday, Thursday	Friday, Saturday, Sunday	
Wednesday, Thursday	Friday, Saturday, Sunday	
Wednesday, Thursday	Friday, Saturday, Sunday	
		Daily—After every shower
Saturday		
	Saturday	
		Daily
		Weekly
		Weekly

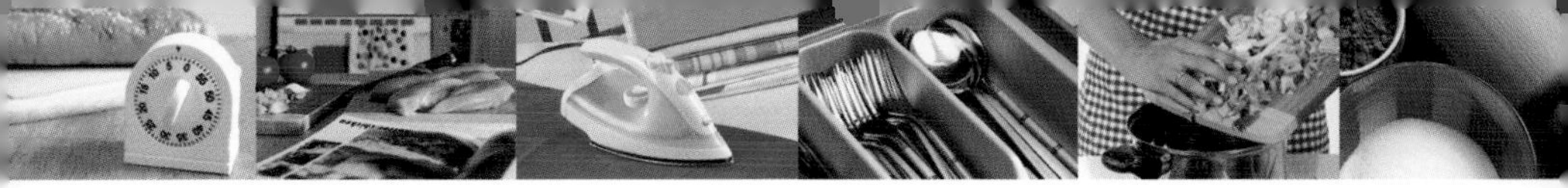

CHAPTER **2**

Understanding Directions on Cleaning Products

Ty spilled a glass of cranberry juice on the living room carpet. He soaked it up right away with paper towels. Then he dumped a little laundry soap on the area and rubbed over it with a wet dishtowel.

Ty thought he'd cleaned the carpet properly. But the next day, he realized the juice had left a reddish spot. Now what was he going to do?

Read the Instructions—Before You Clean!

The rest of the carpet was clean. So, Ty didn't want to hire a professional service to clean the whole living room. All he wanted to do was remove the spot.

Ty bought a product intended to remove spots from carpets. Before he began to clean the spot, he read the product label, which was on the back of the bottle:

FORMULA 208
CARPET SPOT CLEANER
Cleans a Variety of Tough Stains!

Formula 208 Carpet Cleaner is safe yet powerful. It's effective on a variety of tough spots and stains, including tracked-in dirt, grease, and food spills. It even cleans up the worst messes, such as pet stains, spaghetti sauce, grape/berry juice, and mud from foot traffic. Formula 208 Carpet Cleaner has special ingredients to resist dirt and stains, too. This makes it easier to clean the same area next time.

Fabric Safety: Use only on wool, nylon, and other synthetic carpets. Safe to use on stain-resistant carpets.

Before Cleaning: Test a hidden area of carpet to make sure it's ***colorfast***. Remove loose dirt from the area that needs spot cleaning. For wet spills, blot the area with a clean, absorbent cloth. Then follow the directions below.

Directions: Spray soiled area with Formula 208 Carpet Cleaner. Allow to sit for 3 minutes. Gently blot the area with a clean, ***absorbent*** cloth or colorfast sponge. Repeat as needed. Allow carpet to dry completely. Then vacuum. For best results, use product promptly after the spot occurs. Do not over wet carpet. Some stains will cause permanent damage even after cleaning.

For Larger Areas: Formula 208 Carpet Cleaner lifts out a variety of tough spots and stains. It's also good for cleaning the entire carpet.

CAUTION: Eye ***irritant***. Avoid eye contact and ***prolonged*** skin contact.

FIRST AID: Eyes—Flush with water for 15 minutes. Skin—Rinse with water.

IF SWALLOWED: Drink a glass of water. Call a doctor.

KEEP OUT OF REACH OF CHILDREN.

Colorfast	Absorbent	Irritant	Prolonged
Not losing color.	Able to soak up liquid.	Something that causes stinging, swelling, pain, or other discomfort.	Extended or drawn out.

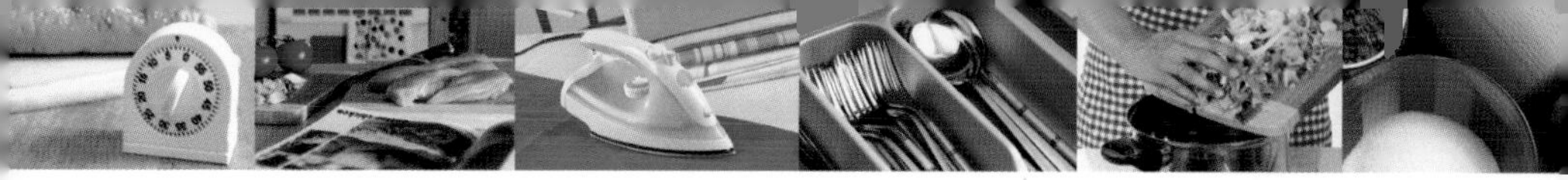

Tips for Carpet Care

1. **Vacuum often**. Keep the carpet clean. Sand and dirt cut the fibers, or yarns, in carpet. That makes it harder to remove dirt and stains.
2. **Catch dirt with doormats**. Place doormats on both sides of entrances—inside and outside.
3. **Remove shoes**. Having a "no shoes" policy will help protect carpet.
4. **Clean stains immediately**. Use a spot cleaner made for carpets. Work from the outer edges of the stain toward the center. Repeat until you can't remove any more. Then thoroughly rinse the area. Dry it quickly.
5. **Use a wet-dry vacuum**. If you have a wet-dry vacuum, use it. It will clean stains more completely. Several rounds of washing and rinsing often are needed.
6. **Vacuum first**. Before deep-cleaning the carpet, vacuum to remove dirt and sand. If you're cleaning the carpet yourself, get the water as hot as possible. And speed the drying time with fans.

Selecting a Vacuum

A vacuum is a big purchase and can range in cost from around $50 to more than $1,000. Before you buy, check out the two main types of vacuums: upright and canister. Know what each does and doesn't do, and think about what features are important to you.

	Upright	Canister
How you use it	Push it in front of you	Pull it behind you
Best use	Good for carpet	Good for bare floors
Good qualities	Good for pet fur Good for large spaces	Multipurpose: cleans stairs, upholstery, and hard-to-reach areas
Bad qualities	Can't get into tight spaces	Not very effective for carpet
Options	May come with attachments for cleaning upholstery and hard-to-reach areas May adjust for cleaning bare floors May use a HEPA (high-efficiency particulate air) filter—good for people with allergies	May come with attachments for different cleaning purposes May use a HEPA (high-efficiency particulate air) filter—good for people with allergies

Selecting Carpet

When you think about selecting carpet, you probably think about choosing a color. But in fact, carpet is made from several types of fibers, or yarns. The type of carpet you buy will affect not only how much it costs. It will also affect how easy the carpet is to care for and how long it will last.

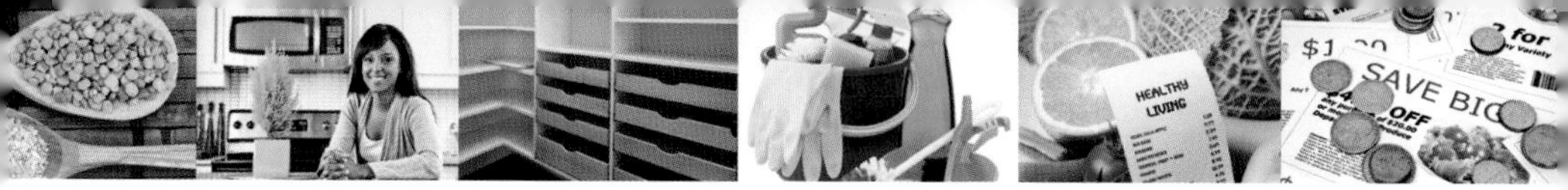

Fiber	Positive Qualities	Negative Qualities
Nylon	Very strong—wears well Fibers resist crushing Dries quickly Resists mildew Cleans easily Inexpensive	Bleaches and fades easily Changes color from pet stains Stains easily
Polyester	Resists bleaching, fading, and soiling Dries quickly	Difficult to remove oily stains Fibers get tangled and matted
Olefin	Resists stains Resists fading Very strong—wears well Cleans easily—bleach and chemical safe	Fibers crush and mat easily Melts easily Friction leaves burn marks Difficult to remove oily stains Shows dirt easily
Wool	Doesn't show dirt Very strong—wears well Cleans well Resists fire	Expensive Stains easily Sensitive to chemicals Dissolves in bleach Fibers fuzz and streak easily

CHAPTER 3

Easy Decorating with Pictures and Plants

Decorating can be fun! You can find lots of ideas in magazines and catalogs and on Web sites and television programs.

Decorating can also be expensive. And after you've just moved into a new home, you may not have much money left over for decorating.

So, be creative! Look for easy and inexpensive ways to decorate. Start by hanging pictures and adding house-plants.

Where to Find Affordable Art

- Look for works of art at yard, garage, and estate sales. Also look at second-hand stores and thrift shops.
- Visit a college or university with an art department. Art students often sell their work at shows or when they need money.
- Check online auction Web sites, such as eBay, eBid, and OnlineAuction.
- Shop Web sites that feature up-and-coming artists. Prices of artworks start at about $20. Start with these sites:

20x200	www.20x200.com/home
The Working Proof	www.theworkingproof.com
Tiny Showcase	www.tinyshowcase.com
We Heart Prints	www.weheartprints.com
Eye Buy Art	http://eyebuyart.com
Society6	http://society6.com

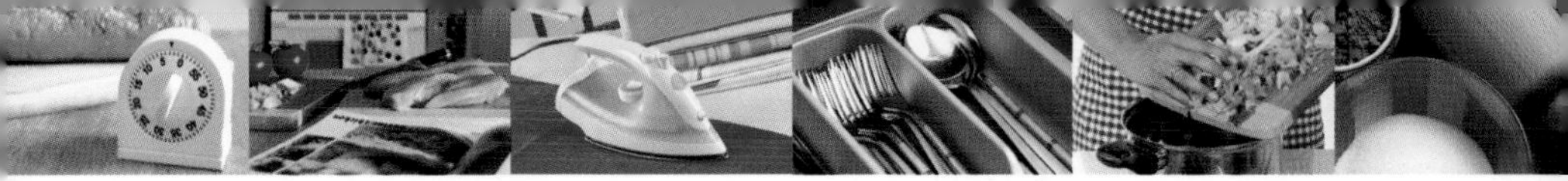

Tips for Hanging Pictures

- Hang paintings out of direct sunlight, drafts, and dampness.
- Don't hang pictures on walls with new ***drywall*** or paint. The dampness may damage the pictures.
- Don't hang pictures above radiators or other heaters. And don't hang pictures on parts of walls with hot pipes or chimney flues inside. The heat will damage the pictures.
- If you want to light up a painting or photograph, use a low-voltage spotlight. Otherwise, keep artwork away from direct sources of electric light. The heat of the lights can damage valuable paintings and photographs.
- For all but the most lightweight pictures, drive the picture-hanging nail into a ***stud***.

Drywall

A type of wall panel made of plaster sandwiched between paper or cardboard surfaces.

Stud

A post inside a wall. Part of the framework or structure of the wall.

- If you want to hang the picture where there is no stud, then use a molly bolt. This type of bolt spreads out inside the wall, giving the picture more support.
- A very heavy frame may need support at the bottom. You can hang a heavy picture so the bottom rests on a piece of furniture. Or you can rest the frame on a ledge or small blocks of wood you've attached to the wall.

How to Frame Artwork

1. **Measure the artwork.** Buy a ready-made frame with an opening slightly smaller than the artwork.
2. **Assemble the pieces.**
   - If the frame has glass, clean both sides of the glass. Then place it in the empty frame.
   - Place the art face down on the glass.
   - Place the backing board on the art. (This piece of mat board comes with the frame.)
3. **Secure the pieces in place.** With the frame/artwork still face down, position three small brads (thin nails) equal distances apart along each side. Using a hammer, tap the brads sideways into the back of the frame. Leave half of each brad sticking out over the backing board to hold everything in place.

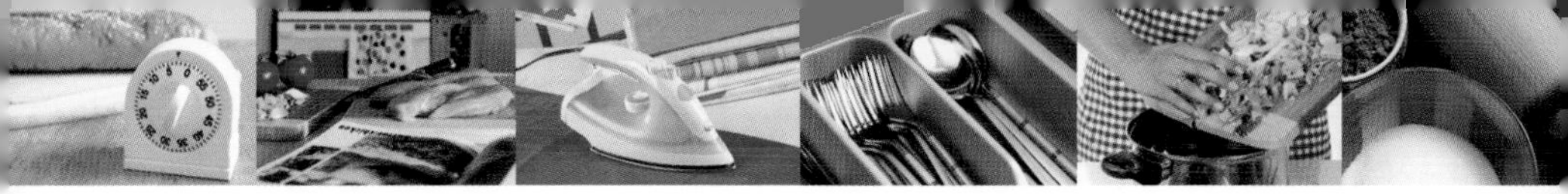

Tips for Taking Care of Houseplants

- All plants need light. But not all plants need the same amount of light. Find out what's good for each kind of plant you have. Then, place each one closer to or farther from a window, according to its needs.

- All plants need water—but again, in different amounts. Some plants need to have damp soil at all times. Other plants need the soil to dry out between waterings. Look up each plant's watering needs, and water it accordingly.
- Some plants need regular misting, perhaps having their leaves dampened daily. For these plants, buy a spray bottle and keep it handy. But don't mist plants near furniture that might be damaged. Take plants to the kitchen sink or outdoors, if needed.
- Plants don't like to be dusty. Use a clean cloth to gently dust off their leaves. A soft brush also works well for this purpose.
- Regularly remove dead leaves and flowers from plants. Doing so keeps them healthy and makes them look better.
- Repot plants that get too big for their pots. If you notice roots growing out of the bottom of the pot, the plant needs a bigger pot.
- Feed plants regularly. Get a good houseplant food, and follow the directions on the label. Some food can be added to the water used for watering. Other plant foods can be added directly to the soil.

Easy-to-Grow Houseplants

Type	Needs direct light	Needs indirect light	OK with any light	Water how much	Feed how much	Main features
Christmas cactus			X	Every two weeks	Every two years	Blooms in winter
Rex begonia	X			Every two weeks	Every spring	Colorful leaves, medium size, ideal for table
Shamrock plant		X		Once a week	Once a year	Blooms almost year round
Pothos			X	Every two weeks	Every spring	Has long, trailing vines
Spider plant			X	Once a week	None	Blooms occasionally
Norfolk Island pine	X (but not too close to a window)			Once every week or two	None	Evergreen, grows up to nine feet tall
Areca palm		X (near a window)		Every two weeks	None	Tropical plant with feathery leaves, grows up to seven feet tall

CHAPTER **4**

Repairing Walls, Paint, and Wallpaper

No matter how careful you are, the walls of your home will get damaged with daily use. Many small signs of wear and tear can be easily fixed, however.

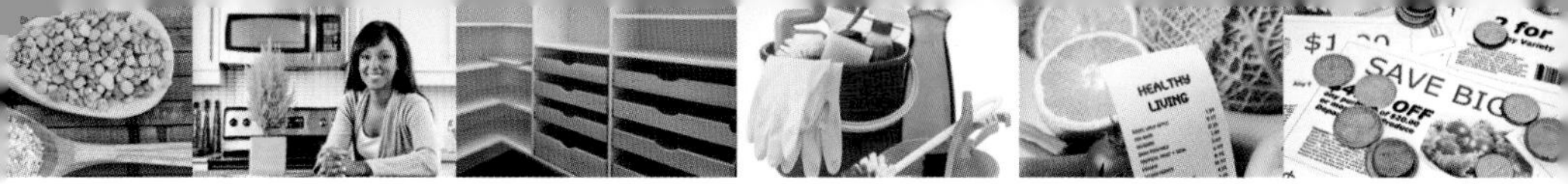

Repairing Wall Damage

Small nail holes and ***gouges*** in drywall can usually be filled. Use an all-in-one nail hole patch product or a joint compound, and apply it with a putty knife. In either case, fill the hole, and allow the repair to dry. Then sand the area smooth with a medium- to fine-grit sandpaper.

For larger holes, you may need to purchase a drywall repair kit from your local hardware store or home improvement center. Before using the kit, remove any loose paper or material around the edges of the hole. Then apply the patch, following the manufacturer's instructions.

Touching Up Painted Walls

Some wall repairs and stains will require paint touch-ups. For a stain or scuff, first try washing the damaged area. Use a sponge or clean rag and plain water, a mild dish soap, or a wall-cleaning solution.

If you need to paint over the area, follow these guidelines:

- Find the original paint, if possible. If it's not available, find the closest possible color and finish.

Gouge
A rough hole or deep scratch.

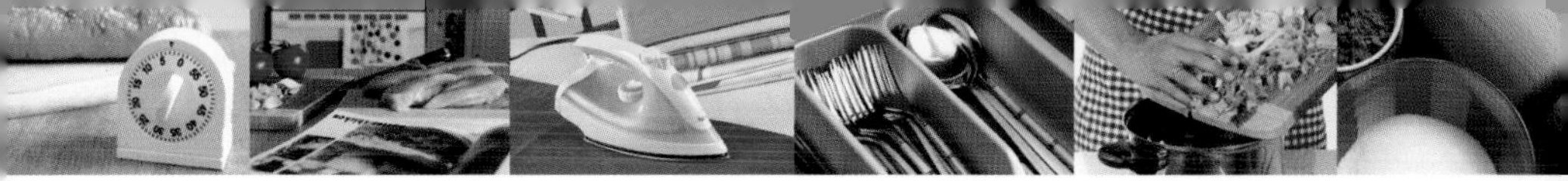

- ***Prime*** the wall with flat latex paint before finishing with a shiny paint. (Flat paint colors are self-priming.) Use sealer to cover stains such as ink and grease.

Prime

To seal or prepare a surface before painting it. Priming wood prevents the paint from soaking in, and priming metal prevents rust from developing.

- Make sure the paint is mixed well. Shake the can or stir the paint just before using it.

Getting Ready to Paint

1. Empty the room, or move everything to the center and cover it with a sheet.
2. Cover the floor with a drop cloth to catch any spills or drips.
3. Fill in any holes and cracks with putty. When they're dry, use sandpaper to smooth the surfaces.
4. Wash walls to remove dust, dirt, and grease.
5. Paint over any stains with a special sealant, so they won't show through the paint.
6. Use painter's tape to mask (seal off) edges around windows, doorways, the floor, and ceiling. This prevents paint from getting into areas you aren't painting.
7. Remove switch plates and outlet plates.

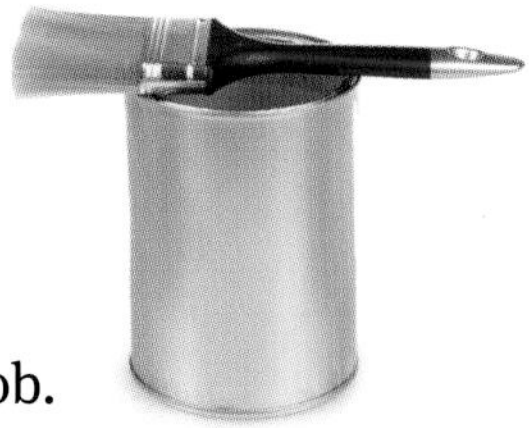

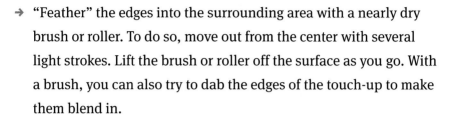

- Touch up the wall using a brush on a small area or a small roller on a large area.
- Before painting the area, try a small test patch first. Let it dry and see how it looks before finishing the job.
- “Feather” the edges into the surrounding area with a nearly dry brush or roller. To do so, move out from the center with several light strokes. Lift the brush or roller off the surface as you go. With a brush, you can also try to dab the edges of the touch-up to make them blend in.
- If there is an obvious difference between the original finish and your touch-ups, you may need to repaint the whole wall.

Repairing Loose Wallpaper Edges and Tears

As wallpaper ages, the edges sometimes loosen or tear. You might notice this problem especially in an older apartment or home.

You don’t have to replace the wallpaper. Instead, use this simple method of repair:

1. For a loose edge, use a wet sponge to moisten the damaged area.
2. Carefully lift the wallpaper away from the wall.
3. Apply a thin, even layer of ***adhesive*** to the back of the wallpaper.
4. Press the wallpaper back in place, and sponge off any excess adhesive.

Avoid soaking the wallpaper, or the adhesive behind it could become loose.

> **Adhesive**
> A glue or other sticky substance used to hold things together.

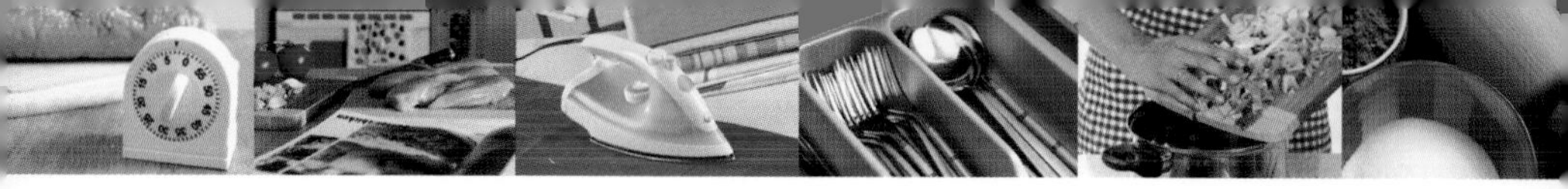

How to Choose Paint

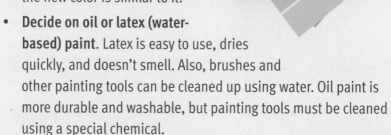

- **Select the color.** Painting a wall is easiest if you choose a color that's similar to that of the ceiling and trim. Using a contrasting color requires greater skill and care to paint straight lines along the edges. Also, fewer coats of paint are needed to cover an old color if the new color is similar to it.
- **Decide on oil or latex (water-based) paint.** Latex is easy to use, dries quickly, and doesn't smell. Also, brushes and other painting tools can be cleaned up using water. Oil paint is more durable and washable, but painting tools must be cleaned using a special chemical.
- **Specify interior or exterior paint.** The two kinds of paint are designed for different uses. Interior paints dry harder, are available in more finishes, and are more washable than exterior paints. Exterior paints are designed to last in all kinds of weather. Also, the chemicals that make exterior paints weather resistant may make them unsafe for indoor use.
- **Pick the finish**: The term *finish* refers to the sheen, or the amount of shine or gleam. Types of finishes range from a soft look with no sheen to a hard look that's shiny and reflective. (See the chart in the box Selecting a Paint Finish.)

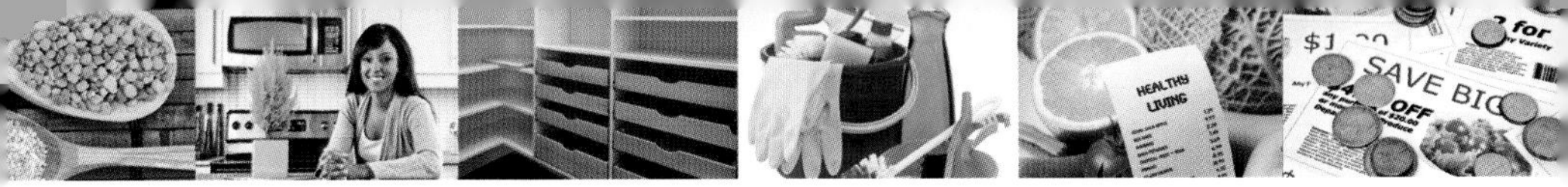

[FACT]

Selecting a Paint Finish

Finish Type	Features	Uses
Flat or matte	Has no sheen Hides wall damage Is the least washable Needs only one or two coats	Ceilings Damaged walls Bedrooms Living rooms Dining rooms
Eggshell or satin	Has a soft, warm sheen Is more washable and stain resistant	Children's rooms Hallways Family rooms Bathrooms
Semigloss	Has more sheen Is more resistant to dirt and scuff marks Is more washable	Kitchens Bathrooms Doors and wood trim
Gloss or high-gloss	The shiniest, most reflective sheen Highlights wall damage Is the most washable and stain resistant Requires the most coats of paint	Kitchens and bathrooms Furniture and cabinets Floors Stairs and handrails High-traffic doors and trim Basements

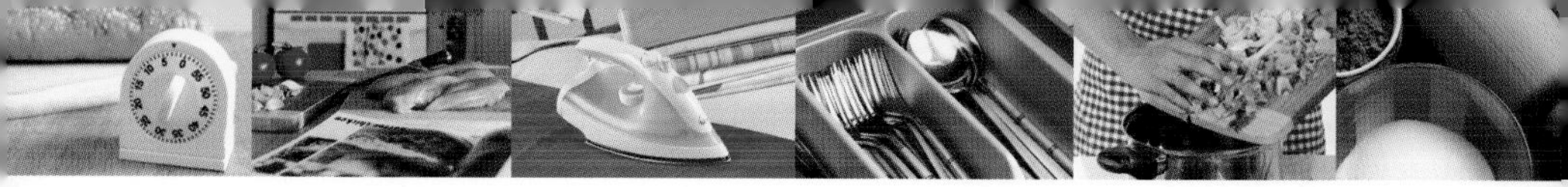

Word List

access
advertisement
aisle
analyze
appearance
appreciate
appropriate
assume
available

bargain
bins
bulk

cabinet
cashier
categories
challenging
chef
chemical
circulate
comparison
conserve
container
convenient
convince
counter
coupon
crease
creative

damage
damp
definite
detergent
determine
develop
device
diet
dimensions
disaster
discourage
divide
dry-clean
drywall
durable

effective
elastic
energy
environment
equipment
excess
expensive
experienced
expiration
exterior

fabric
fantastic
finish
flavor
fragile
fragrant

gadget
garment
glamorous
goods
grains
groceries
guidelines

hangers
herbs
household

inexpensive
infrequent
ingredients
injury
insect
instructions
intend
interior
invisible
irregular

laundry
liquid
logical
low-fat

Word List

maintenance
manufacturer
measurement
menu
microwave
moisten

name-brand
negative
nonstick
normally
nutrition

obvious
ongoing
online
organize
overview
overweight

package
pantry
particular
perform
permanent
popular
portion
possibilities
previous
process
produce
product
professional
promptly
properly
protect

qualities
quality
quantity

rarely
ready-made
recipe
recommend
related
repair
repeatedly
replace
requirement
responsibilities
responsible
rotate

schedule
seasonal
section
select
serving
shelves
shipping
simplify
slightly
soak
specific
spoil
stain
staples
storage
substitution
subtle
supermarket
supplies
sustainable

technique
temperature
texture
thermometer
thorough
thrifty
time-saver
traces

unit
utensils

vacuum
variety
vocabulary

willing

Index

Index

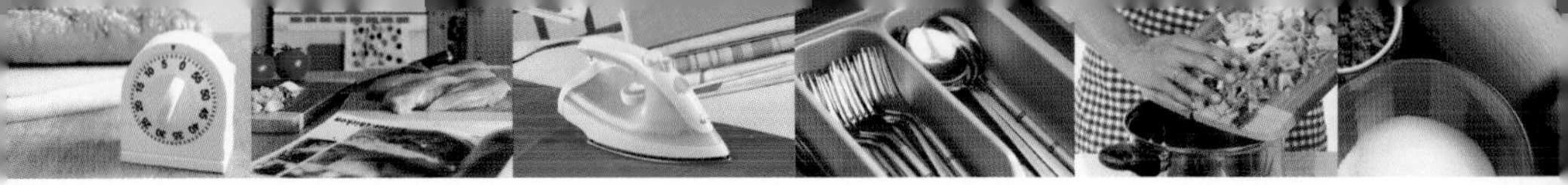

Index